Spirituality for the Challenged

Spirituality for the Challenged

By Matthew Paquette, MD, MTS

Published by Matthew Paquette

Copyright © 2024 by Matthew Paquette
All rights reserved.

ISBN: 979-8-218-51877-6

Except where otherwise noted, all biblical quotations are taken from *The Holy Bible*, Revised Standard Version; Second Catholic Edition (San Francisco: Ignatius Press, 2006).

Excerpts from the English translation of the *Catechism of the Catholic Church* for use in the United States of America Copyright © 1994, United States Catholic Conference, Inc.—*Libreria Editrice Vaticana*. Used with Permission. English translation of the Catechism of the Catholic Church: Modifications from the *Editio Typica* copyright © 1997, United States Conference of Catholic Bishops—*Libreria Editrice Vaticana*.

TABLE OF CONTENTS

Preface _____ i
Introduction _____ 1
1 The Spiritual Life: Summary _____ 5
2 Modernism _____ 9
3 Who is Man? _____ 20
4 Who is God? Part I: Mercy _____ 34
5 Who is God? Part II: Covenant _____ 46
6 Testimony _____ 52
7 Sacraments _____ 59
8 Distrust of self _____ 62
9 Confidence in God _____ 67
10 Proper Use of Faculties _____ 70
11 Prayer _____ 83
12 Polycrisis _____ 94
13 Hope _____ 102

Preface

This book is written in the style of a retreat. In other words, it is not written in the style of a formal text, but rather, as if I were having a personal conversation with you, the reader. I chose this style for many reasons.

First, I find books written in this way the easiest to read. I am a slow reader to begin with, and much slower when the author is very technical and writing about difficult concepts. I don't have to work so hard to understand books written like this one.

Second, I do this every day. When I see patients, I explain medical concepts in a way that makes sense to them no matter who they are. When I discuss theology or philosophy or whatever with family or friends, I use words and images that they can relate to. I am able to do this because I remember how hard it was for me to learn all of these things in the first place. It would have been so much easier for me to learn these things if someone had explained them in an easier way.

Third, this is the way the Bible was written. God speaks to us in ways that we can easily understand. As Mark Twain once said: "It ain't those parts of the Bible that I can't understand that bother me, it is the parts that I do understand."

Some people may not like this style of writing. That is OK. My goal is to try to explain God's Infinite Love for each of us, the infinite worth of every human soul, and all of the gifts that God has given us to restore union with Him.

As you will see, it is the ultimate irony that I am writing this book. Understanding spirituality, the interior workings of the spiritual life, and actually praying have been more difficult for me than medical school. None of this has come naturally for me. I have needed more help than anyone I know. My goal is to pass along some of that help to anyone who could use it.

Introduction

Spirituality has always been a challenge for me. I will discuss these many challenges throughout the book. I want to address two of them here, at the beginning, because they are two themes that run throughout the whole book. Some people seem to simply understand these issues and take them for granted. I was not so gifted.

The first issue I want to address is location. Whenever I think about anything going on inside of us, I first think of location (anatomy), then how that part is supposed to work (physiology). Then, like a mechanic, I try to figure out what went wrong (pathophysiology/disease) and how to fix it (treatment).

Spirituality

Before locating spirituality, a definition would be helpful. Definitions are always helpful because they explain to us exactly what we are talking about. *Our Sunday Visitor's Catholic Encyclopedia* defines spirituality as "[T]he response of the individual, by the grace of the Holy Spirit, to Christ's ongoing invitation to 'repent and believe in the Gospel.'"[1] But this definition doesn't give me an image of where it is located.

---

[1] *Our Sunday Visitor's Catholic Encyclopedia*, Revised edition, ed. Peter M. J. Stravinskas (Huntington, IN: Our Sunday Visitor, 1998), 933.

The Heart

Its central location, I came to learn, is the "heart." The *Catechism of the Catholic Church* (*CCC*) describes the heart as "our hidden center, beyond the grasp of our reason and of others.... The heart is the place of decision, deeper than our psychic drives. It is the place of truth where we choose life or death. It is the place of encounter...it is the place of covenant."[2] The heart, therefore, is where we can meet with God, and where God can dwell/live in us.

The heart is the center of our spirituality, but all of our other parts are involved as well. Spirituality involves all of our parts and every aspect of our lives. When we choose "life," it means that our desires and decisions are based on what God wants (because God always wants what is best for us). When we choose "death" (sin), we put our own desires and decisions ahead of God's. Since spirituality involves the totality of our lives, then an introductory book on spirituality should address all of the major aspects of our lives.

Imagination

The second theme that runs throughout the book is the imagination. When I returned to spiritual reading at fifty-five years old, I was blindsided by

---

[2] *Catechism of the Catholic Church* (hereafter *CCC*), 2nd ed. (Vatican City: *Libreria Editrice Vaticana*, 1997), 2563.

the importance of the imagination. Since much of the spiritual life is invisible, there is no device that can visualize "the heart." There is no instrument that can measure love. The Holy Spirit leaves no footprints when He is present. My eyes cannot see the life of the Trinity dwelling inside of me when I am in a state of grace. I can't quantify my desire to know, love, and serve God. We can't see Infinity or Eternity. Because of this, I will offer many images throughout this book that have helped me use my imagination to "see" the invisible realities.

It took a while for my math and science brain to get used to this. Then I thought about quantum mechanics, numbers themselves, dark energy, etc. Electromagnetic waves (radio waves and others), for example, are passing through us constantly. We are completely unaware of this and many other invisible realities. So, there is much in the natural world that is invisible as well. We certainly study these invisible entities and create images of them.[3]

Guides

Perhaps, the greatest value of this book will be to point you in the direction of some of the best guides

---

[3] The obvious question that I do not address in this book is *how* we create images of invisible things. The answer is that, while these things are invisible to the eyes, they are "seen" by reason and, because of this, can be converted into images to represent those things. It would, however, be beyond the scope of this writing to examine the process by which we convert ideas into images.

in the spiritual life. I am certainly not one of them. My goal is to try to build a map to give you a lay of the spiritual land. Hopefully, then, when reading any spiritual author, you will better understand his vocabulary and know roughly where to place him in the map. This is the book that I needed at age twenty.

Map of Life

Centuries ago, when most of the West was Christian and most people were farmers, a map of life was part of their day-to-day existence. It was taken as a given that God was above all and created all. They depended on God for day-to-day help. They experienced the circle of life every day and every year.

Now, we have lost our narrative as Christians. We no longer see ourselves as part of the continuous river that is salvation history. Further, what fills our atheistic culture is often artificial and disconnected from our deepest needs. So, we need to be reminded of our place in nature as well.

The map I will draw will be limited by the small space of a few chapters (2–5). But it will include what is most important in life. It will include the essentials. It will include the invisible realities that make up the spiritual life. It will include Reality Itself (God) because everything that exists is because of and contained within Him.

1
The Spiritual Life: Summary

You shall love the Lord your God with all your heart and with all your soul, and with all your mind. This is the greatest and first commandment. And the second is like it, you shall love your neighbor as yourself. On these two commandments depend all the law and the prophets
(Mt 22:37–40).

This chapter is a type of Cliffs Notes. I like Cliffs Notes because I can't understand any trees without seeing the forest first. Unless I know where each tree in the forest fits in, unless I know the context for anything, it doesn't make sense to me. The rest of the book is a footnote to this chapter.

The spiritual life can be boiled down to the above quote. That's all we have to do. We have to love God as the highest love of our life and we have to love our neighbor as ourselves. Implied in this is that we have to love ourselves as profoundly as God loves us.

But what God makes simple we make complicated.

Loving God above all else is our biggest challenge. When Cecil B. DeMille was filming the movie *The Ten Commandments*, someone asked him which commandment he thought was most frequently broken. He didn't hesitate: "The first one. We are idol-making machines." We turn our houses, cars, sports, screens, gyms, food, alcohol, drugs, politics, even our anger, into idols. We love them more than we love God. The proof? Where do we spend our money and what do we do with our free time?

We find it hard to love our neighbors. Even our friends and family, whom we love more than others, are difficult to love sometimes. And loving our enemies is an enormous challenge of the Christian life.

At times (and for some of us, most of the time), loving ourselves is extremely difficult. We are not kind to, or forgiving, of ourselves. Sometimes we hate ourselves and won't let go of this hatred. We focus on what we should be rather than who we are right now (a person who is not yet perfect, but at least trying to be). We don't see ourselves as beloved children of God the Father Who can't take His loving eyes off of us and Who loves each of us with an Infinite Love.

Three Enemies

But it was not this way in the beginning. God did not create suffering. We created suffering when we disobeyed God. So now, the simplicity of the spiritual life (love of God, neighbors, and oneself) is extremely complicated. More than that, it is a constant battle. "The 'spiritual battle' of the

Christian's new life is inseparable from the battle of prayer" (*CCC*, 2725). There are three enemies in this battle: the world, the flesh, and the devil. We will try to understand these enemies in the next two chapters.

If we are to have any chance at victory in battle, we must have a plan.

First, we can never lose sight of our goal: love of God and neighbor.

Second, we need to remember that God wants us to win. God is not just a bystander on the battlefield. He not only wants us to win, but gives us every weapon (Grace) we need in order to win.[1]

Third, we need to know ourselves: both our strengths and our weaknesses.

Fourth, we need to know our enemies: the world, the flesh and the devil. Over time we will learn their tactics and how best to fight each battle.

Fifth, we need to know there will be losses (sin). We are not yet perfect; indeed, most of us have a long way to go.

Sixth, we always, always have to get back up after sin, confess the sin, and see every confession as a new beginning. God makes all things new, including us. We need to trust in His Goodness and never stop begging for His Mercy. Remember, God's favorite thing to do is to forgive sins.

---

[1] See Eph 6:10–20.

Sin as Sickness

The Eastern Orthodox use a medical analogy to describe this reality. Spiritual health is loving God above all things and loving our neighbors as ourselves. God made Adam and Eve with perfect spiritual health. Sin makes us spiritually sick. Original Sin means we are all born ill. Christ, the Divine Physician, came to heal us of our worst illness—sin. This too is a good summary of the spiritual life.

To continue with the medical analogy, the first half of the book is an overall diagnosis of our condition right now. The second half is the treatment plan.

2
Modernism

Modernism is the summation of all heresies.
Pope St. Pius X

Like an adolescent rebelling against a parent, early modern civilization had formulated its beliefs in inherent contrast to everything the parent had held dear.[1]
Thomas Goldstein

Men have forgotten God.[2]
Aleksandr Solzhenitsyn

The world has been a source of temptation for everyone since the fall of Adam and Eve. In simpler times, stealing, adultery, murder, etc., were real temptations and actual sins. But never before in human history have temptations been so numerous and attractive. World travel brought spices, ceramics, new foods, luxurious fabrics, etc., to the West. The combustion engine and electricity made travel and home life even easier. But now with instant global communication of any content (including, very commonly, perversions that are beyond most people's wildest imaginations), we are

---

[1] Thomas Goldstein, *Dawn of Modern Science* (Boston: Houghton Mifflin, 1984), 250.
[2] Aleksandr Solzhenitsyn, Acceptance Address for the *Templeton Prize for Progress in Religion*, May 10, 1983.

tempted all day and night in ways our ancestors couldn't imagine. So, the battle against the world is the same, but temptation is now more attractive and easier to find.

But there is more to the story with our first enemy, the world. It is something more sinister than nonstop distraction.

Almost everyone I know has a deep sense that something is very wrong in our culture. Some say they don't know what is going on, others blame one issue or another, still others blame politicians. There is much confusion because the rate of change is so rapid. And the changes are resulting in a decline of our culture at every level (moral, intellectual, spiritual).

What is behind all of this? Is there one thing or many things? Is it all by historical accident, or are there people and ideas pushing these changes? I wrestled with these questions for years. Not knowing how we got here and where we are going made me uneasy and anxious. The mind rests in truth, but is restless with confusion.

After years of reading and help from many smart people I was able to make some sense of how we got here. My goal in this chapter is to help people get a rough outline of our recent history. By doing so we can get a better idea of how our culture was shaped and continues to shape each of us. On a spiritual level, I also hope that this awareness will shed light on how we see God, and help us to better conform our view of God to the beauty of Who He is.

Luther

For the sake of space, we will start with Martin Luther (1483–1546). Almost all Christians in the West were Catholic until 1517 when Martin Luther started his own church, the Lutheran Church.

The Catholic Church stands on three pillars: Scripture, Tradition, and the Magisterium. The Magisterium is a long continuous line of succession of bishops that started with the twelve apostles. They are the teaching authority and the administrative body of the Church. The Magisterium officially gave us the Bible in the year 382 at the Council of Rome. Tradition with a capital "T" consists of "the apostles who, by their oral preaching, by example, and by observances handed on what they had received from the lips of Christ, from living with him, and from what he did, or what they learned from the prompting of the Holy Spirit"[3] Tradition is not an invention of the Catholic Church. God's people, Israel, had both a written and an oral tradition before the Church was founded by Christ.

When Martin Luther established his own church, he removed Tradition and the Magisterium. One of his major tenets was "Scripture alone." This

---

[3] Vatican II, Dogmatic Constitution on Divine Revelation, *Dei Verbum* (November 18, 1965), 7.

was a critical juncture in the history of the West because he got rid of Tradition and the concept of a universal authority here on earth. As a result, many people no longer looked to the Church and Her Tradition. Our attention was now focused on ourselves and on the future (progressivism). Put simply, the future would no longer be shaped by the past. Everyone, for example, could produce their own interpretation of the Bible.

Thirty Years War

The Thirty Years War in Europe (1618–1648) saw Protestant Christians fighting with Catholic Christians. It was fought to a stalemate, and by the end, all of Europe was exhausted and broke. Many became disillusioned with a belief system that saw so much killing among fellow Christians.

Newton

In 1681, the Englishman, Isaac Newton, came on the scene. His *Principia* was probably the greatest scientific publication of all time. Suddenly the movements of nature could be described mathematically. His laws of motion set the groundwork for what we know as modern science. Actually, he was standing on the shoulders of many giants before him (Galileo, Copernicus, etc.), but his was a great breakthrough.

Newton's discoveries came at a time when Christendom was exhausted and depressed. People had become disillusioned, Protestantism had already broken into many pieces, and there was no central authority to settle disputes nor Tradition for guidance (among the Protestants, at least). Other heresies were being spread within the Catholic Church as well. Where is truth when so many disagree about Truth? People started to look to science with great excitement. Suddenly the secrets of nature were being discovered. These were solid truths that could be demonstrated with experiments. These were solid truths that would lead to greater advances in science. These were truths that would greatly benefit the daily lives of many. And they didn't cause people to start wars.

If Newton (and others before him who paved the way for modern science) had made his discoveries four hundred years earlier, the natural sciences would have probably remained in their proper domain. But at that time in history, Europe was looking for a change. And change they did. We are still living in the midst of that change.

Enlightenment

The Enlightenment (1700s) quickly followed, bringing a whole new approach to philosophy and politics. There were many currents of thought other than modern science that led to the Enlightenment (so called "Age of Reason"). And the Enlightenment was different things to different people. But the underlying sentiment of revolt was evident throughout. The intellectual spirit of revolt started by the Enlightenment then became actualized in physical revolts.

Civil War

What began in the U.S. in 1776 spread throughout the whole world for the next one hundred and forty years. Civil wars popped up all over the world. Back then nations were ruled by kings who had central authority over the whole nation. Technically, in many cases they also owned everything. A major aspect of these civil wars was "anti-authoritarian." So, at first, it was monarchies that were being toppled. But the people who took control were almost always worse and more authoritarian than the former king (with the U.S. being about the only exception). Communism is a case in point. And the cycle of political revolt continued.

Atheism

As time went on, the revolts spread. What began with revolt against the Church (1500's) progressed to the philosophical and political arenas (1700's), and then turned against the Bible and God Himself in the 1800's. People had been working very hard for many years to discredit Scripture and promote disbelief in God. They finally found their hero and advocate in Charles Darwin, whose book *On the Origin of Species* was published in 1859.[4] Our culture in the West has not been the same since.

In sum, Darwin's theory says that all life on earth is here by random chance. All life on earth got here first by coming into existence by random chemical interactions, and then one species changing (evolving) into a higher species, and so on. We call this idea "macroevolution," meaning one species changing into another species. "Microevolution," on the other hand, is when changes take place within a species; it is something obvious that we can see every day. This is what breeders do; they breed certain animals within a species to get offspring of the same species with certain characteristics.

This is not the time or place to refute Darwinism. Many others have done so in ways better than myself (e.g., Michael Behe,[5] et al.). If

---

[4] See Donald De Marco and Benjamin Wiker, *Architects of the Culture of Death* (San Francisco: Ignatius Press, 2004), 75: "In fact, evolutionary theory was always part of the larger materialist view of Epicureanism and was reintroduced into the West through the discovery of the Epicurean texts in the fifteenth and sixteenth centuries." Epicureanism was an ancient Greek philosophy that viewed pleasure as the highest good.
[5] See, e.g., Michael Behe, *Darwin's Black Box: The Biochemical Challenge to Evolution* (New York: The Free Press, 1996) or his more recent book *Darwin Devolves: The New Science About DNA That Challenges Evolution* (New York: HarperOne, 2019).

Darwin proposed his theory today with what we know (fossil evidence, DNA, cell structure and function, etc.) he would be laughed out of the room. The evidence strongly disproves his theory. Furthermore, it is statistically impossible. And people conveniently ignore the second law (not theory!) of thermodynamics, which says that all things tend toward disorder. But the atheists who shape our culture continue to prop up the theory as truth because it is their bedrock foundation.

Thomas Goldstein paints an accurate picture of our culture today in the West:

> The modern world...originated in a fierce revolt against the pressures of traditional Medieval civilization. The source of modern history has been radically shaped by that revolt, which is, in a way, still going on and of which we are still a largely unconscious part.[6]

Our culture is fundamentally Darwinistic (atheistic), whether we acknowledge it or not. The Christian worldview has been pushed out of the public square, and is now being persecuted to various degrees. Our laws are grounded in utility and raw power rather than a transcendental moral code. Darwinistic evolution is being taught as an indisputable truth from kindergarten through graduate school. Those who question Darwinism

---

[6] Goldstein, *Dawn of Modern Science*, 246.

will not receive research grants or tenure or anything but scorn from their colleagues. The news media takes evolution as a given. So being born and raised in our culture scars each of us, to varying degrees, with this unspoken but presumed atheism. At some level and to some degree (except for the few mystics) all of us see the world as a place that is not infused with God or able to be influenced by Him.

Natural Law and Nature

A summary of our current atheistic culture is that for the past five hundred years our culture has been in a state of revolt. What started as a revolt against religious authority progressed to a revolt against political authority, then against Divine authority, then against the authority of the Natural Law, then against nature itself. The sexual revolution, with subsequent contraception, sterilization, and abortion, was a revolt against the Natural Law. We are now in the final stage of revolt, against nature itself. We are not only in revolt against our own biology (transgenderism) but against life itself. Transhumanism, where we are coupled with a computer, is rapidly becoming a reality. Genetically modified seeds and organisms are altering the fabric of nature. We are in the final frontier of this very long-standing and progressive revolt.

Loss of Sense of Sin

Perhaps worst of all—but as a logical conclusion—we no longer see sin as sin. If God does not exist, and there is no such thing as Natural Law, then there is no standard for morality. And if there is no standard for morality then there is no infraction against that morality; i.e., there is no such thing as sin. Pope Pius XII observed this deterioration back in 1946 when he said, "Perhaps the greatest sin in the world today is that men have begun to lose the sense of sin."[7] And, if there is no sin, there is no need for a Redeemer. So, the whole Gospel message is no longer Good News but no news at all.

I mention all of this for a few reasons.

First, we are all born at a particular time and in a particular place. It is helpful to see that time and place for what it is. This gives us a degree of awareness about the lens through which we view the world, God, and our spiritual life. It shapes our worldview.

Second, the promises of modernism have not only come up empty; they have turned our lives into a nightmare. Its champions promised (and still promise!) great freedom and human flourishing if we can only get out of the shackles of God and organized religion, with its restrictive morality. Yet, the attempts to liberate us from God and organized

---

[7] Pope Pius XII, Radio Message to Participants in the National Catechetical Congress of the United States in Boston (October 26, 1946).

religion in just this last century have been an overwhelming disaster and produced widespread misery. Atheistic regimes of the twentieth century have caused the deaths of over one hundred million people (not counting the abortions). Depression and anxiety are epidemic in the West (but not in third world countries). Suicide is epidemic. Drug abuse is epidemic. Slavery (human trafficking) is epidemic. Divorce is epidemic. Abortion is epidemic. And, these epidemics have resulted in a severe poverty right here in the midst of plenty. That is why Mother Teresa once said "I have never seen such poverty as I have seen in the U.S."

So, we in the West—if we approach God at all—approach Him as revolutionaries, whether we know it or not. I talk to many people who—if they think of God at all—think of Him as a cruel tyrant. Hopefully this chapter explains where some of that negativity toward God is coming from.

Obviously, modernism has brought us many great benefits. I can't imagine life without running water, sewers, and antibiotics for starters. We need to be very thankful for all of these great benefits, but a house built on sand (without God) will be washed away.

3
Who is Man?

The glory of God is man fully alive.
                                    St. Irenaeus

For you are dust, and to dust you shall return (Gen 3:19).

[M]odern science ... is moving towards the supernatural with the rapidity of a railway train.[1]
                                    G. K. Chesterton

The spiritual life is the interior life. The interior life is where God interacts with us and where we interact with God. But just as the spiritual life influences (or should influence) every other part of our life, the relationship goes the other way as well. Every other aspect of our lives influences our spiritual life. Knowing the basics of our interior parts, how they work and how they interact with our interior life will be extremely valuable information.

The term for the basic parts of our interior life is Christian anthropology. It literally means "the Christian study of the human person." I had this class at thirty-three years of age; it was possibly the most helpful class I have ever taken. My classmates agreed. We all wondered why this wasn't common

---

[1] Gilbert K. Chesterton, *Orthodoxy* (New York: John Lane Company, 1909), 275.

knowledge, why it wasn't required learning for everyone. After the class, we finally had an understanding of how we all operate on the inside.

Hierarchy of Being

If we want to understand a human being, or anything, it is helpful to see it in its full context (how it relates to everything else). There exists what we call the order of being. The highest being is God Who is Being Itself. God is Existence Itself. God is Pure Spirit, i.e., He has no body. As a pure spirit, He must possess the highest kinds of activity of intellect and will; therefore, God is a Person.

Next in this hierarchy of being are the "angels" (which literally means "messengers") or "intellectual substances" as the pagan philosopher Aristotle called them. They too are pure spirits and without bodies. They too possess intellect and will and are persons. Like God, they have the power of reason and they have freedom.

Human beings are next. Like God and angels, human beings possess intellect and will and, therefore, are persons; so, too, are we spiritual. But unlike God and angels, human beings also have a physical body. As a composite, we are, as it were, midway between heaven and earth; we inhabit an eternal world with God and the angels and physical world with the animals. We are a hybrid of sorts.

Next, we have the animals. They are alive which means they have a soul. They have a physical body animated by what we call a sensitive soul. Since, however, animals do not possess intellect or will, they are not person and cannot inhabit an eternal world.

The second to the lowest position in our hierarchy belongs to plants. Plants are alive and have a physical body. They sense their environment, seek nutrition, and reproduce, but their ability to react with their environment is quite limited when compared to animals. In short, they do not possess locomotion. Therefore, they are not animated as animals are and only have what is called a "vegetative" soul.

The last being in our hierarchy of beings belongs to simple material beings like rocks. Inanimate matter does not reproduce, seek nutrition, grow, sense, etc., and, therefore, purely material beings have no soul and are not alive.

As we can see in the above, there are levels of being and, within this hierarchy, there exist levels of souls. The soul is the principle that gives life to a body. It is what leaves the body or simply ceases to exist at the time of death. The soul animates the body. Vegetative souls direct the growth, maturation and reproduction of the plant. Sensitive souls do everything the vegetative souls do, plus the powers of locomotion and more awareness of their surroundings. When these souls die, they are gone forever. Rational souls in humans have all of the powers of the lower levels plus the power of reason and freedom. Our intellect has the power to transcend the limitations of matter. We can think about things that are not immediately present and we can think about higher things like just and peaceful relationships. Our will exhibits the power of freedom. Conversely, non-rational beings, especially inanimate matter, must strictly follow the laws of physics. Plants and animals follow their inscribed patterns and instincts. In the physical world we alone have the freedom to behave in whatever way we choose, for better or for worse.

Humans

When trying to get an idea of how all of this fits together, a picture may be worth a thousand words:

Human Anatomy

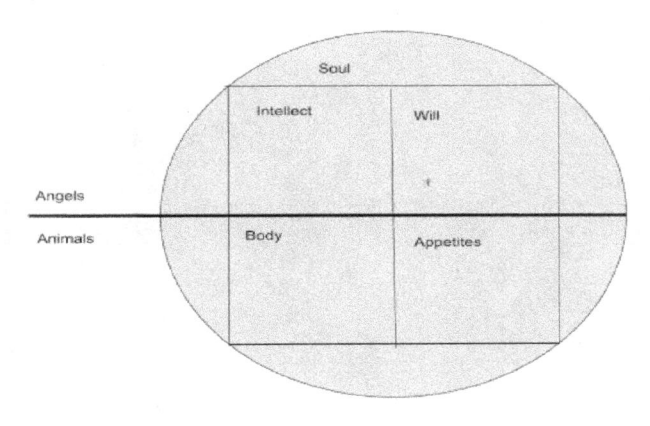

	Soul	
	Intellect	Will
Angels		
Animals	Body	Appetites

We are a spiritual being with a body. Our rational soul is what makes us spiritual. And all rational souls are eternal. Our soul animates every part of our body, so I drew a circle encompassing our human nature. The heavy line across the middle distinguishes our physical nature below the line from our spiritual nature above the line. We share the lower half with the animals and the upper half with the angels. The "heart" is "located" in the depth of the soul. The soul is present in all of our parts, but it also has a deep, hidden part. Again, the heart is "our hidden center, beyond the grasp of our reason and others ..." (*CCC*, 2563).

The above diagram depicts our "anatomy" or the parts of our soul. Our physiology/psychology is how the parts interact and work together. In this case it is not simply our physical parts but our spiritual parts as well. So properly termed it would be "psychology" (which originally meant "the study of the soul). Here is how we were made to function:

Physiology/psychology

Intellect	Will
Body 5 senses	Appetites

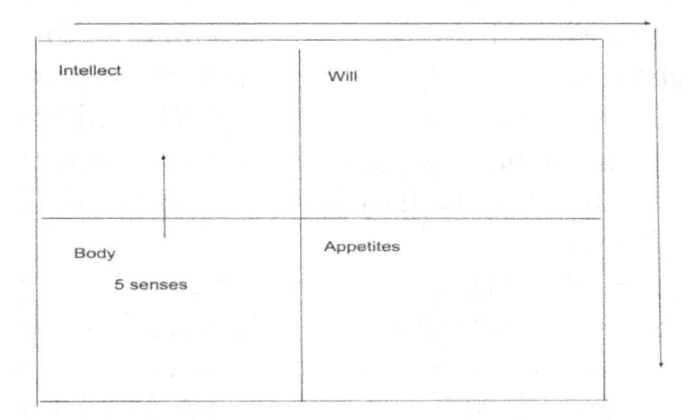

Our five senses collect data from the world around us. All of our data input is from the five senses. This data is sent to the intellect. The intellect extracts truth from the image presented to it. The intellect decides what is good and presents this to the will as desirable. The will then chooses to desire this good and not others, and then tells the lower appetites to pursue and do the good.

An example would be learning that chips are unhealthy and that vegetables are healthy. Health is a good and should be pursued. The intellect tells the will that health is a good thing and that vegetables are good for health. The will then tells the lower appetites to desire and eat vegetables and to avoid chips. Then you would actually eat vegetables and avoid chips.

Every decision was this way before Original Sin. God made us to live this way. The term for always choosing the proper good is *integration*. Adam and Eve were fully integrated before Original Sin. They ate when they were hungry. They didn't overeat or undereat. They didn't sleep too much or too little. Etc. That is, they had full control of all of their faculties.

Original Sin has been devastating and, as a result, we no longer have full self-possession; we are no longer integrated. St. Paul said as much in his Letter to the Romans: "For I do not do what I want, but I do the very thing I hate" (Rom 7: 15). We no longer have full control of our faculties. This lack of control includes not only the acquisition of our basic necessities of food, water, sleep and reproduction. It includes the higher functions of intellect and will as well. A lack of control in the higher functions results in things like greed, envy, malice, gossip, etc., as well as excessive or inordinate behavior regarding screen-time, drugs, sports, cars, and clothes. The list could go on. We are a mess. Again, a picture can help:

Pathophysiology/abnormal psychology

Intellect	Will
Body	Appetites

Instead of our highest power (intellect) directing our lower powers (appetites), our lower powers are directing our higher parts. What distinguishes human beings from the animals is the power of reason. Now, however, the powers we share with the animals are directing our higher, spiritual powers. This is obviously disordered. This is why St. Paul can say: "For the mind set on the flesh is death, but the mind set on the spirit is life and peace, because the mind set on the flesh is hostile to God." (Rom 8:6–7).

Suffering

Before Original Sin we were not only integrated internally, we were in harmony with God, with each other and with nature as well. Original Sin broke this unity at every level. We lost the life of the

Trinity dwelling within us. We also became conflicted with each other, and at odds with nature. God unites. Sin divides. The goal of the spiritual life is to restore our original harmony with God and within ourselves.

It is important to note here that God did not create suffering. All of our suffering, in one way or another, can be traced back to sin—Adam and Eve's, our own, or that of others. There was no suffering in the beginning. Sin leads to suffering. Suffering is not from God. Suffering is a form of evil, and God cannot create or will suffering for us.

It is also important to note here that God did not abandon us. In fact, His plan to rescue us was HIMSELF suffering and dying for us. We have a loving Father—the model of all fatherhood—the one Who loves His children so much that He will suffer and die for them.

As the ideal Father, God is also the best Teacher. He knows what we need even if we don't. He gives us what we need, even if we don't like it. And sometimes He asks us to suffer, not for ourselves but for others. We want to eat dessert and junk food all day (i.e., we want to sin and not suffer). He allows us "healthy food" (suffering), not because He wants to harm us but because He wants to help us. Suffering is meant to purify us, for the redemption of others, and to draw us closer to Christ. His one goal for us is to get us back into full union with Him. The absolute proof of this is the Cross.

Elephant in the Room

We want to believe all of this. We really do. But this can't be true. There is no evidence of a "Garden of Eden." It is not consistent with what we know about the history of the earth. And it's not possible that God created two human beings out of the blue. We know that man has evolved, and we even know the later stages of that evolution.

And so, all Christians living in the post-modern West, to some degree or other, live in a state of cognitive dissonance (the state of holding inconsistent thoughts or beliefs). We are taught from day one in school that evolution is a fact. All of our thoughts and ideas about human beings are framed by evolution. Evolution forms the context of our thinking about human beings. This cognitive dissonance among Christians today is the elephant standing in our spiritual rooms. Some of us are aware of it, many are not. But it is one of the many unrecognized causes of the anxiety and unease that is afflicting Christians today. God made us to rest in the peace of truth. Truth is symphonic, internally consistent and cohesive, not contradictory.

This cognitive dissonance is also one of the causes of our epidemic of practical atheism.

> A particularly dangerous phenomenon for faith has arisen in our times: indeed, a form of atheism exists which we define,

precisely, as "practical," in which the truths of the faith or religious rites are not denied but are merely deemed irrelevant to daily life, detached from life, pointless. So it is that people often believe in God in a superficial manner, and live as though God did not exist.[2]

Darwinism

The theory of evolution is radically opposed to the Christian message. The human soul is not natural but supernatural. Every human soul is directly infused by God at the time of conception. Adam and Eve were created by God as the only two people at the beginning of humanity. Non-humans (or any other creature) cannot gradually attain a rational soul. A human soul does not come about gradually. It is either there or it isn't because God has to infuse every human soul. So, if there were other people gradually attaining a human soul, original sin would not exist. And if original sin does not exist then baptism is meaningless. And, if we don't need baptism, then Jesus died in vain. Darwinism negates the entire Christian message.

Darwinism is the greatest threat that Christianity has ever faced. There is no full-frontal attack and it is not political. It denies the vertical

---

[2] Benedict XVI, General Audience (November 14, 2012).

(spiritual) dimension of life. It is subtle and seemingly objective. It is very deceptive because it is actually a worldview masquerading as scientific theory. But if you dig deeply enough into it you realize that it takes a greater leap of faith to believe in Darwinism than it does to believe in the God of Jesus Christ.

How has the Church responded to Darwinism? Many popes since 1859 have condemned it. One outstanding example is the encyclical *Humani generis* by Pope Pius XII promulgated in 1950. I quote a small portion:

> [E]specially today, when we see the principles of Christian culture being attacked on all sides.... Some imprudently and indiscreetly hold that evolution, which has not been proved even in the domain of natural sciences, explains the origin of all things.... Communists gladly subscribe to this opinion so that, when the souls of men have been deprived of every idea of a personal God, they may the more efficaciously defend and propagate their dialectical materialism.[3]

More recently, Cardinal Joseph Ratzinger, the future Pope Benedict XVI, called Darwinism a "cruel ethic" due to the eugenics that directly follows in its

---

[3] Pope Pius XII, Encyclical *Humani generis* (August 12, 1950), 1, 5.

wake.[4] And, it could be that his assessment was merely an echo of Darwin himself who famously prophesied:

> At some future period, not very distant as measured by centuries, the civilized races of man will almost certainly exterminate and replace throughout the world the savage races.[5]

Indeed, eugenics is a very cruel ethic. Darwin's theory has had horrific consequences. And we know this tree by its fruit.

This is the perfect time to explain the Church's position on these issues. The Church claims to be an expert in only two areas: faith and morals. The issue here is one of Faith. The Church insists that we assent to everything She teaches with respect to faith and morals. We don't need to understand everything She teaches. But we need to take a leap of faith and believe it (like not understanding the rules of your parents when you were young, later realizing the wisdom in them). Our intellect does not need to fully grasp Church teaching. But we need to acknowledge it as truth because of Who revealed it—God Himself. Then the intellect needs

---

[4] This assessment was made by Cardinal Ratzinger in a talk given at the Sorbonne in Paris on November 27, 1999. The talk was later reprinted in his book *Truth and Tolerance: Christian Belief and World Religions*, trans. Henry Taylor (San Francisco: Ignatius Press, 2004), 178–83.
[5] Charles Darwin, *Descent of Man and Selection in Relation to Sex*, Part I, ch.6 (Princeton University Press, 1981), 201.

to tell the will that it is good. The will then needs to desire it as a good.

In other words, we have to believe that God made Adam and Eve as separate and distinct from the rest of creation. If God can make the Big Bang to begin the universe, He is certainly capable of creating two human beings to begin the human race. He infused a rational (eternal) soul into one man and one woman at the beginning of the human race. We have to believe that they were fully integrated (without sin) in their Original Condition. They were in communion with God (in a state of Grace) and with each other. We have to believe that they did sin and lost the peace of their original integrity. Here is one instance of many when repeatedly using our imagination to imagine this will be helpful.

4
Who is God?
Part I: Mercy

God, infinitely perfect and blessed in himself, in a plan of sheer goodness freely created man to make him share in his own blessed life (CCC, 1).

See what love the Father has given us, that we should be called the children of God; and so we are (1 Jn 3:1).

I have called you friends, for all that I have heard from my Father I have made known to you (Jn 15:15).

Usually when I talk about God, I start with the personal. I talk about His Love and Mercy first and foremost, which is a good place to both start and finish because love and mercy are His greatest attributes. And since all of us are broken by sin, what we need first and foremost is His love and mercy.

But I would like to say something about God's other attributes first, for three reasons. First, they will make His love and mercy even more amazing, and give us greater appreciation of them. Second, I hope that a better understanding of His attributes will increase our fear of the Lord. Fear of the Lord, in its essence, is awe and wonder. When persons as small as ourselves come into contact with the Infinite, we are bound to be overwhelmed. Third, our secular mindset gives us no reference points of how to think about God. Hopefully this will be helpful.

Eight Divine Attributes

Thomas Aquinas teaches us that God has eight attributes.[1]

The first is *infinity*. God has no limits. As with all of His attributes, we have no reference point that comes close to us being able to imagine this. The best we can do is to consider the universe. The universe is estimated to be 95 billion light years across. Since one light year is 5.88 trillion miles, the universe is 540 sextillion miles across. This is 54 followed by 22 zeros. I don't know if anyone can really imagine how big this is, but I can't. Yet the whole universe is like a tiny grain of sand in the hand of God (to use an image from Scripture that we can understand). There is no end to God.

The second attribute is *simplicity*. This just means that God is not composed of separate parts.

The third attribute is *ubiquity*. God is everywhere. Everything that exists exists within God.

---

[1] Thomas Aquinas, *Summa theologiae*, I, QQ. 3–11.

The fourth attribute is *unicity*. God is the One Thing, and everything that exists is from Him and in Him.

The fifth attribute is *indivisibility*. God is an undivided unity.

The sixth attribute is *immutability*. God does not change. His creation changes, but the Author of creation does not change.

The seventh attribute is *spirituality*. This means that He has no body. He is Pure Spirit.

The eighth attribute is *eternality*. Eternity, like Infinity, is way beyond our imagination. The biblical scholar Jeff Cavins paints us a tiny picture of this. Imagine taking a grain of sand off of Mount Everest every million years. By the time the mountain was gone, Eternity would be just getting started.

Can anyone even begin to imagine that a God Who is Infinite and Eternal would lower Himself to be a speck of dust like ourselves? It doesn't seem possible. It doesn't make sense. And yet He did it. And then He died by the cruelest torture. This is why Jesus was folly to the Greeks and a stumbling block to the Jews. Who can blame them? People in the know couldn't see Jesus for Who He was because it didn't make any rational sense to them. It didn't seem remotely possible to them.

The Logic of Love

So how do we make sense of the Incarnation, Death, and Resurrection of Jesus? Our fallen human reason is unable. Only through the eyes of faith can we make sense of this. Therefore, we have to turn to God to hear His explanation.

Everything that God has done and continues to do for us makes perfect sense when we understand the "logic of love."[2] The logic of love says that I will do anything— ANYTHING—to restore union with my beloved. The logic of love says that I define my happiness by perfect union with my beloved. This makes little sense to us because we operate under the logic of sin.

In order to understand the logic of love we would do well to start at the beginning. God is love. Love is the total gift of self to the beloved. God created us out of love. He created us because love is effusive. Love wants to keep giving and expanding and growing. It is never static. He made humanity and put us in the Garden of Eden. There was no pain, no suffering, no death, no disease, no shame, no hunger or thirst. And it was climate controlled (i.e., there was no unreasonable excess of heat or cold). Not only were all of Adam and Eve's physical needs provided for, without effort, they were fully integrated. In other words, there were no

---

[2] Pope Benedict XVI, Angelus (September 24, 2006).

compulsions, addictions or false idols. They were perfectly ordered internally. Adam and Eve were at peace within themselves, with each other, with God, and with nature. They could do whatever they wanted except ONE thing. As we know, they did the one thing, and lost the whole Garden.

It turns out that original sin was not eating a piece of fruit from the one forbidden tree. Original sin was disregarding God's authority and claiming authority for themselves. God created everything, so He has the authority (which is always out of love and for our benefit) to declare what is good and what is evil. In their pride, Adam and Eve decided on their own to declare what was good and what was evil. They trusted themselves rather than God. Their view of good and evil was opposed to God's. They disobeyed, they sinned.

Suffering

When Adam and Eve sinned, they lost more than free food, climate control, and a life without suffering and death. Sin divides. We were now divided against God, divided amongst each other and at odds with nature. But we were now also divided within ourselves. They lost integration within themselves. So now we are burdened by not only hard work and lots of pain, and we have lost control of our desires. And our disordered desires cause us more pain. So, the cycle continues.

Now, living with all of this pain and suffering, we see God as a tyrant, indifferent, or we see Him in any number of negative ways. But as we said earlier, God does not change. So, what happened? We changed. We rejected God. We failed the test. God still loves us with the exact same love. But now that we have rejected that love, after the easy way, we have to learn how to love the hard way. Ever since Original Sin, our path to love is through suffering. Jesus' Passion proves this point, and gives us the Ultimate example.

Why is suffering the only way? Because love is the total gift of self to and for the beloved. We no longer have the ability to give ourselves completely to another because we don't have enough self-possession to do so. We are no longer integrated. We don't have a total self to give. We have a fractured, broken self. So, even if we do decide to love someone completely, we are unable. We are at war within ourselves—struggling with selfishness, compulsions, addictions, idolatry, etc. Someone at war within himself does not possess the fullness of himself. So, when we decide to love someone, we can give him or her as much of ourselves as we possess and of which we are in control, but we are unable to give more. So, our love is imperfect. Because our love is imperfect, we suffer and so do all those around us.

If I could be granted one wish, it would not be to win the lottery, to be famous, to be a great athlete or to be a genius. My one wish would be that everyone on earth would understand the meaning and value of suffering. "If the angels were capable of envy," wrote St. Faustina, "they would envy us two things: one is the receiving of Holy Communion and the other is suffering."[3] Consider how the Navy Seals see their training, Olympic athletes see their exercises, professional musicians see their practices, or graduate students see their studies. I don't think that any of the above mentioned enjoy all of the suffering that goes into making them great. But they want to be great, so they choose to suffer long and hard.

The saints do the same thing, but it is not for their own glory. They do it because they know that an ever-deeper love with their Beloved and for the salvation of souls (i.e., love of neighbor) requires further purification or suffering. I know a woman who has been wheelchair-bound her whole life. She is one of the most joyful people I have ever met. She offers up all of her suffering for the Church on earth. I imagine her having a very high place in Heaven.

But suffering for the sake of greatness is not an adequate explanation for it. The problem of suffering, the problem of evil, is probably the greatest challenge to Christianity. This challenge

---

[3] Kowalska, Maria Faustina, *Diary of Saint Maria Faustina Kowalska: Divine Mercy in My Soul* (Stockbridge, MA: Marian Press, 2005, 2014), a. 1804.

comes not only from the outside (non-Christians) but also from the inside. The Bible's Book of Job is a case in point.

All Suffering is from Sin

There are four reasons for suffering. All of them are because of sin. The first two are due to Original Sin in general. We just discussed the first. We were made to love. But because of Original Sin we are unable to love as we ought. So, the process of getting to the point of total self-gift is very painful. But Original Sin did not just introduce division into our personal faculties. By losing residence in the Garden of Eden we are now vulnerable to hunger, heat, cold, infection, and every kind of illness and death. All of these general forms of suffering can be traced back to Original Sin.

The second two reasons for suffering involve personal sin. Our own sins cause us suffering. The sins of those around us also cause us to suffer. Sin divides. Sin weakens. Sin causes harm. We know this all too well from personal experience.

An example of this would be slander. Slander is when someone tells a damaging lie about another person. This lie harms the reputation of the person who was lied about. It also hurts the person who lied, making them untrustworthy. It also hurts all of the people around them if those people are seen in a more negative way and the general trust of the community is diminished.

We can say all of this, and it makes sense. But in the midst of extreme suffering, we can't make sense of it. Some types of suffering strike to the core of our being. We can hardly breathe. This can go on for years. Pope Saint John Paul II said many things about suffering in his encyclical *Salvici doloris* (*SD*), promulgated February 11, 1984. It is the best work on suffering anywhere by anyone. At the end of the day, "Love is also the richest source of the meaning of suffering, which always remains a mystery" (*SD*, 13).

God as Merciful Father

As always, God has the answer to our questions and problems. An adequate explanation brings us to the center of this book, the center of our hearts, and the center of God Himself. God is our loving FATHER. Possibly the most shocking thing that Jesus said was "Pray, then, this way: 'Our Father …'" (Mt 6:9). The words roll off of our tongues and we usually don't think much of it. But everyone before our atheistic age had some sense of the greatness of God. He had to be at least as big as the universe. How could He be bothered with a tiny human? How could He care about me personally? He has a lot of other things to care and think about. How could we, as tiny specks of dust, refer to Him personally as our Father?

The Prodigal Son parable (Lk 15:11–32) has been called the greatest story ever told within the greatest story ever told (i.e., the story of Jesus Christ). This parable best expresses the Heart of God our Father. This parable best expresses the logic of love, of which we spoke.

Out of respect for his son's free will, the father let him leave with half of the father's fortune. What the son did while he was away was the worst-case scenario for a first century Jew. He rejected his family, his religion, his homeland, and his moral code. Sin always ends in misery, and eventually the son felt the full weight of his sin. How does the father respond after losing half of his fortune, being slapped in the face by his son, and humiliated in front of all of his neighbors?

Well, the father's heart ached for his son. He wasn't happy without him. Love for his son won't let him rest until he is reunited with him. He watches for him day and night. How do we know this? Well, with a little help from the swine and slime, the son eventually "came to himself," repented of his wicked ways, and returned home, and "while he was yet at a distance, his father saw him and had compassion, and ran and embraced him and kissed him" (Lk 15:20). First century Jewish men did not run or leave the house to greet people. He hugs and kisses his son. His son was unclean, which would have made the father unclean. Which meant he couldn't worship. He gave his son the family ring, which meant he was officially a full member of the family. Then he throws a huge expensive party to celebrate.

This parable gives us a glimpse into the Heart of our Father. But it doesn't tell us how much the father suffered while his son was away. We can infer that his heart was agonized to the point where he could barely go on.

The only story better than the parable of the Prodigal Son is the real story of Jesus Christ. God lowered Himself from Infinity to live among us. His own children tortured Him to death. The reality of this story tells us that God will do anything—ANYTHING—to be reunited with us. He can't stand to be apart from us. The only thing keeping us apart from Him is sin. And He came to take away that sin. We simply need to repent and accept that forgiveness.

The story of Christianity is too outlandish to make up. If it wasn't real, nobody would believe it. Nobody could defend it. Christianity is ridiculous to anyone who only operates by the logic of sin. The logic of sin is strict justice without mercy (if someone else gets caught). The logic of sin is to sin whenever we want as long as we don't get caught (if we are the ones sinning). The logic of sin is to write laws that allow sin. It's also consistent with the logic of sin—though ironic—to imagine that we can't or won't be loved after we sin.

Conversely, once our eyes are opened to see the logic of love, everything that God has done and continues to do makes perfect sense. And it's more wonderful than anything we could have possibly imagined. But it always involves suffering for this short time here on earth.

One more important note about the Passion: we see it as the outpouring of love that is more than we could ever imagine. But there is a flip side to the torture and death of Jesus. It is a visual image of the horror of sin. Jesus took the sins of all of us upon Himself. Sin disfigures us. Sin tortures us. The worst part of sin is that it cools (venial sin) or breaks off (mortal sin) our relationship with God. That is why God takes sin so seriously. God can't stand anything that gets in the way of our loving union with Him; He can't stand being apart from us. He gave us the Ten Commandments not to take our fun away but to keep us united to Him.

That is Who God is.

5
Who is God?
Part II: Covenant

[Y]ou are fellow citizens with the saints and members of the household of God, built upon the foundation of the apostles (Eph 2:19–20).

The spiritual life is centered on God. And when Christians think "God" they should also immediately think "Church." The *Catechism* reminds us that "The world was created [by God] for the sake of the Church" (*CCC*, 760), and that the Church is the Family of God.[1] The biblical word for family relationship is also "covenant." Whenever God establishes a special relationship with a person or people, He calls it a covenant. In the New Testament, the word for Family (of God) is Church. New Testament (the good news of Jesus Christ and His Church) is another word for New Covenant. But understanding the Old Testament roots of this is critical here.

Covenant

Whenever God chooses a people to be Family (His chosen people), He makes a covenant with them. A covenant is not a contract, which can be broken. A covenant is a blood oath that signifies a family

---
[1] See *CCC*, 759.

bond. The blood part of the oath means blood must be spilled to seal the covenant. Something (or Someone) must die. The blood signifies family (who share the same blood). It also signifies the death that will result if one side breaks the covenant.

Examples are helpful. When God made a covenant with Abraham, a goat, a ram, a turtledove, and a pigeon were cut in half.[2] When God made a covenant with Moses, oxen were sacrificed. Half of the blood went to the altar and the other half sprinkled on the people.[3] When the Israelites made covenants with neighboring peoples, the same ritual was followed. If either side broke the covenant, they would be killed. Covenants were and are deadly serious.

Jesus came to expand the Family of God beyond the children of Israel (who had been scattered over the centuries). He also came to fulfill all that He had promised to Israel. But nobody—nobody—in their wildest dreams could have imagined that it would be God Himself Who would visit the earth physically. And beyond that wildest dream nobody—NOBODY—could have dreamed that God Himself would spill His own Blood to establish the New Covenant. "Drink of it, all of you; for this is my blood of the covenant, which is poured out for many for the forgiveness of sins" (Mt 26:27–28).

---

[2] See Gen 15:17.
[3] See Ex 24.

God takes Family so seriously because He loves His children so much. He loves us like the father in the Prodigal Son story, and He proved it by pouring every drop of His blood out for us, so that we could enjoy the deepest Family bond with Him. More than that, He wants His children to love each other as family. The father in the Prodigal Son story wants the older brother to love his younger brother. God created the family. The first commandment that God gave to Adam and Eve was "Be fruitful and multiply" (Gen 1:28). (One of the reasons the demons hate us is because God gave us the power to co-create with Him—reproduction—but He did not give that power to the angels.) So, we can look to our families on earth as an analogy. We do not have children merely to have a one-on-one relationship with each of them. We hope that each of our children experiences the love for each other that we the parents have for each of them. Together we are family. Within the family, the parents indeed have a unique relationship with each of their children. They love each of them equally but differently, and they also want their children to love each other.

I am saying all of this for two main reasons. First, I want to continue offering images that can help us spiritually. The family image fits so well because it is a true image. Second, this helps us to understand the two dimensions of the spiritual life: vertical and horizontal.

Who is God? Part II: Covenant

God First

The vertical dimension of the spiritual life is first and foremost. As Christ Himself reminds us, "Apart from me you can do nothing" (Jn 15:5). The vertical dimension is God actually condescending to us and living inside of us (when we are in a state of Grace). God comes to us not just to restore order to our disordered faculties, but to actually dwell within us. God the Father wants that kind of intimacy with us, with His children. He wants us to be completely united to Him. This is the one-on-one relationship of a Father with His children.

Neighbor Second

The horizontal dimension of the spiritual life is the fruit of God's life within us. This is the children of the Father loving and taking care of their siblings. God has given each of His children a certain set of gifts. He has done this brilliantly so that we all have something to give to the Family of God, and so that we all truly need each other. God made all of us unique and distributed His gifts among us so that we, in turn, can be gift to each other. And our siblings are all gifts to us, even though we sometimes would rather have not received one particular gift or the other. Many families with handicapped children say that the handicapped child was the greatest gift to the family. It was the glue that held them together, forced them to work more as a team and to expand their love.

All of this discussion on family is to help us see the Reality we are entering into when we develop our spiritual life. We are entering into the Life of God. The Life of God brings us every good gift. It is glorious beyond our wildest dreams. But for this short time on earth, it always involves suffering. It involves suffering because we are living in Christ, which means we are part of His Body. "He is the head of the body, the church" (Col 1:18). When we live in Christ, we share every aspect of His life. And His life included great suffering.

Entering into the life of God means being part of a Family (which is now called the Church). This makes perfect sense because God is our common Father and He created us to be social beings. This is difficult, as family life often is, but it is also wonderful at many levels. First, we are part of something bigger than ourselves. Second, it forces us out of selfishness. Family dynamics are not healthy when one or more members are working for themselves and not for the team. Getting rid of selfishness is always painful, but it is a good and necessary form of suffering. Third, it helps us to grow in love. This is the goal of the whole project/pilgrimage here on earth.

With these images and goals in mind we can more easily see the value in the daily battle. The spiritual life is a continual battle for love and against selfishness. If we can see the big picture, that the prize at the end is much greater than any Olympic gold medal, we can hopefully persevere (even joyfully) to the end.

6
Testimony

I often share my story with patients. They find it helpful in dealing with their conditions. Maybe you will find it helpful as well.

I have struggled in my spiritual life for many reasons (beyond the usual sins). I have had severe generalized anxiety since I was born. I was adopted. Many did not believe I struggled this way until they met my adoptive aunts. They said that as a baby I would cling for dear life to whoever was holding me. I don't remember an hour of my life without anxiety. God lifted some of this anxiety from me at age 25. If He hadn't, I would not have been able to see patients. Unfortunately, I did not see this for the miracle that it was at the time. I squandered that Grace on dissipation. After that, the anxiety again worsened.

I have also struggled with shame most of my life. Some define shame as not believing that we are worthy of love and belonging. Our most basic need as humans is love and belonging. So, shame is an agonizing belief that strikes to the core of who we are. Growing up I knew my parents loved me, but I didn't think I could be lovable unless I was perfect. Perfectionism is one response to shame. So, I couldn't fully experience my parents' love in my heart. The same was true with God. I knew that He was Good and Trustworthy for other people, but surely not for me. It is said that the furthest distance in the universe is the distance between the head and the heart. It was certainly true in my case.

I have had ADHD since puberty. Unfortunately, I was not diagnosed until about the age of forty. I didn't have enough self-awareness to try to figure out why I couldn't focus or study. Knowing the diagnosis was very helpful, but treatment is still a challenge.

Furthermore, I have an addictive personality. It was either zero beers or 10 beers, no screen time or four hours straight of screen time, no ice cream or a quart of ice cream. I thought this was normal until I talked to a nurse who was divorced. She said that after the divorce she tried to become an alcoholic but couldn't do it. I couldn't relate to or even imagine this. For many years, my wife and I believed that we could not overcome our addictions. (I have heard many testimonies on the radio recently that many others have had the same thought.) For years we fought them and fought them. Then suddenly one day they were gone. Obviously, it was Grace at work. I love the many different ways that God shows us His power and His healing in our lives.

For me, the worst aspect of my impediments was that I couldn't see them for what they were. First of all, I didn't have any formal diagnoses, so I didn't have a name for any of these conditions. I literally didn't know what I was dealing with.

Secondly, I didn't have enough self-awareness to analyze these conditions on my own to try to make some sense of them. Thirdly, I had too much shame to ask for help. Fourthly, my head was constantly buzzing with either the worry at hand or the possible worry of the future. I couldn't think. I couldn't be with myself and calmly try to figure things out. Because of this internal chaos (I call it a storm cloud), I had no self-possession. It goes without saying that I had no internal life to speak of. If the spiritual life is the internal life, and is our most important work on earth, I was in big trouble.

The road of spiritual progress has been long and hard, both for me and those around me. I have had huge breakthroughs on healing retreats. My wife has been a godsend. One of my former theology professors has spent countless hours helping me to clear many of the spiritual roadblocks that remained. Now, I am fifty-eight years old, and finally making progress in my spiritual life. But is it really true that I made no progress for twenty years?

We have said that the spiritual life is the interior life. The fruit (outpouring) of that interior life takes many forms, but can be summarized as love of neighbor. The interior life is centered in the heart. And the heart is the place where we choose life or death (God or sin). But the heart is also "beyond our reason" (*CCC*, 2563). So, even though I was not aware of any interior life to speak of, my spiritual life had grown by leaps and bounds. I did not perceive much difference between who I was at age thirty-eight and age fifty-eight. All of my prayers were the same. If anything, I felt myself to be worse off spiritually, and frustrated that I hadn't advanced at all. In reality I prayed consistently, grew in love and was less selfish. Extremely painful circumstances for years on end forced me to either love more or turn to hatred. I chose love and so was able to advance, though without my being able to see it. When life is overwhelming, it is like the fog of war. We can't always see things clearly for what they are, including our progress.

Here is where we begin to dissect the heart. I am a beginner in this area, but I will tell you what I know. I was extremely grateful to learn that Teresa of Avila, John of the Cross, and Thérèse of Lisieux stand out as the three authors over the past two thousand years who best describe the inner life. This was extremely valuable information. Now I could focus on their writings with this in mind. I was taught that, despite their popularity, it took four hundred years for their writings to be systematized. The two volumes, *I Want to See God* and *I Am a Daughter of the Church* by P. Marie-Eugène of the Infant Jesus contains this synthesis.[1] This was a huge breakthrough. I finally found the two books

---

[1] Marie-Eugène of the Infant Jesus, *I Want To See God* and *I Am A Daughter Of The Church*, tr. Verda Clare (Chicago, IL: Fides Publication Association, 1955).

that best describe the anatomy and physiology of the heart.

Back to the point at hand. I perceived no difference in my interior life for over twenty years. But great progress had been made. When we continue to choose life over death, when we continue to repent after our seemingly endless sins, when we choose to love our neighbors (all of them), then we are growing in union with God. We are advancing spiritually. We can't do any of this alone. We need God's help every step of the way. And we can be assured that He Himself is not only alongside us but within us at work helping us at all times and in all places. So, even if we do not perceive His presence or notice any improvement within ourselves, we need to trust that He is at work in us. He is our Spiritual Director. He wants what is best for us and will always help us to fulfill that best plan.

There is more to the story. After the dust cleared from several years of intense pressure (a child in crisis, then caring for people during COVID), I was finally in a place where I could start to better see my heart as it was. I finally realized that God has called me to do much more than what I am capable of doing. I have been broken. I have been broken because I love my family and I love my patients. But my mental state did not give me the emotional capacity to love all of these people in the way that

God has called me to love them. When you give more than what you have, you break.

Why did God do this to me? God allowed me all of this suffering because He loves me. God loves me so much that he wanted to purge me of my greatest sin: pride. If He would have called me to this same life but made things easy for me, I would be extremely arrogant. I would be judgmental, and I'd wonder why everyone else can't get their life together. I would not be able to walk with people who are struggling like I can walk with them now. I would not be capable of loving people to the degree that I can love them now. I would not acknowledge my reliance on God as I do now. I need Him for everything. Everything.

Now don't get me wrong, pride is still lurking around every corner. And I fall into various sins, all day, every day. But, thanks be to God, the main forest of sin is cleared. There is much more to clean up, but much progress has been made.

There are three very important points to this story. The first is the value of suffering. There is no shortcut to clearing the forest of our sin. There is no shortcut to humility (the foundation of the spiritual house). There is no shortcut to wisdom. Suffering is necessary for our purification and spiritual growth. Please read the Bible's Book of Sirach, Chapter 2, until you feel it in your bones.

The second point is that our spiritual growth often remains hidden in our duties of daily life. I had no idea all those years, in the midst of all the chaos, that growing in love and getting less selfish was actually a huge spiritual development. I had no interior life to speak of, but I was making great progress in the second of the two great commandments (love of neighbor). We can and do become saints by fidelity to whatever vocation God has called us to in life.

Third, when it comes to prayer, there are seasons in life when all we can do is show up. God understands. He can't expect more. He doesn't demand more than what we have to give. I have made huge spiritual strides since this roadblock was cleared from my spiritual life. I felt hamstrung spiritually for many years. I went to Mass every day. I said my rosary and chaplet every day. But I felt like I was blocked spiritually. I knew that there was something missing, but had no idea what it was or how to fix it. When I heard that there are times when all we can do is show up, it was a great relief for me because that was all I was capable of doing for years on end. The growth during that time was invisible to me. And I can tell you that God greatly rewards that fidelity to prayer. Patience and perseverance are virtues, and only developed in long suffering.

Hopefully we now have some idea of who we are and how we got here. The second half of the book will be a treatment plan that I have collected from some of the best experts.

7
Sacraments

By his power [Christ] is present in the sacraments (CCC, 1088).

The sacraments are essential, critical, vital to the spiritual life. The sacraments are portals of Grace whereby the whole life of the Trinity enters into us. The sacraments get us into the Family of God, keep us in the Family of God, and give us what we need along the way to help us live out Family life.

Baptism

Baptism is what gets us into the Family of God. All human beings are made, known, and loved by God. But since the Original Sin, we are all born without the life of the Trinity dwelling within us. Baptism removes Original Sin from our souls and infuses the life of the Trinity into our soul. This is our spiritual adoption into the Family and we are now in a state of Grace.

The words "State of Grace" describe the state of our soul when God is dwelling there. We should be thinking of this every day. When we are in a state of Grace, we are spiritually alive. We have access not just to faith, hope, and love (supernatural virtues—we cannot get these on our own) but also to the seven gifts of the Holy Spirit (supernatural wisdom, understanding, knowledge, counsel, fortitude, piety, and fear of the Lord). Possession of God Himself in our soul should be our most prized possession. We should be afraid of losing it (by way of mortal sin). We should thank God continually for it.

We are spiritually dead before we are baptized and after mortal sin. This means that the life of the Trinity does not dwell within us; we are spiritual zombies. God gives life, and without Him we are dead. When we are not in a state of Grace, we lack the help and guidance and strength that only God can give. Our enemies—the world, the flesh and the devil—are much more powerful than we are. We don't stand a chance against them without God's help. We see this on full display today. We wonder how people can believe and follow some of the craziest ideas, things that no rational person would even consider. It should not surprise us because most people in the West today are not in a state of Grace.

Confession

Confession restores us to a state of Grace when we lose it.

Eucharist

The Eucharist is "the source and summit of the Christian life" (*CCC*, 1324). How can the Church say this? The Paschal Mystery (the life-death-resurrection of Jesus) is the Blood that was poured to establish the New Covenant. Each Mass is not symbolic. It is an actual participation in the Paschal Mystery. It is being at the foot of the Cross. The Eucharist "commemorates Christ's Passover, and it is made present: the sacrifice Christ offered once for all on the cross remains ever present" (*CCC*, 1364). How can this be? Well, God exists outside of time and space. Every moment is "now" and every place is "here" for God. All of the past, present and future as we know them are present to God all at once. So, every Eucharist celebrated here on earth is a participation in the Eternal Heavenly Liturgy.

The Eucharist is the source and summit of the Christian life because every aspect of the New Covenant flows from the Blood that ratified that Covenant. Every apostolate, every charism, every sacrament, every vocation, every part of the Christian life has its source in the Blood of the Covenant.

8
Distrust of self

The man who has a deep distrust of himself and places great confidence in God is not at all surprised if he commits a fault.[1]

Dom Lorenzo Scupoli

The spiritual life is all about relationship—Family relationship. And these relationships are based on the law of love. Living in this world ruled by the law of sin, how do we grow in this love? Where do we begin?

The spiritual life has to begin with the vertical dimension. Without God we can do nothing. And God acts in the depths of our soul, our heart. So, the spiritual life begins and ends with the interior life. It is for all, observed the great spiritual master Father Garrigou-Lagrange, "the one thing necessary," and so "ought to be constantly developing in our souls; ... it is the life of the whole man."[2] So, the project of our interior life is our most important project on earth.

When I first heard the above remark, I was shocked. I had no awareness of my interior life. If this was our most important work, I needed to start

---

[1] Lorenzo Scupoli, *The* Spiritual Combat *and* Treatise on Peace of Soul, Ch. 4 (Rockford, IL: TAN Books, 1990 [original Italian 1608]), 17.
[2] Reginald Garrigou-Lagrange, *The Three Ways of the Spiritual Life* (Westminster, MD: The Newman Press, 1950 [original French, 1938]), 1.

moving fast in this direction. But where to start? There are numerous books on spirituality, many of them written by saints. One issue for us today is that most of those authors lived in a monastery hundreds of years ago. The principles are all the same (God has not changed and human nature has not changed). But how we approach our interior life, and all of spirituality in general, is going to look different now based on the radical changes in the world around us.

Our Guide

I am a beginner in all of this, and so I am going to choose a guide to help us with an outline, a structure, an overall game plan for our approach to this in general. The *Spiritual Combat* by Dom Lorenzo Scupoli seems to me a good first guide. It is a short book. It is so good that St. Francis de Sales called it the "golden book," he carried it wherever he went, and he read part of it every day. De Sales is a doctor of the Church in spirituality, so I think we are in good hands.

The *Spiritual Combat* identifies four main pillars in the spiritual life:
- distrust of self,
- confidence in God,
- proper use of the faculties, and
- prayer.

We will address each of these in order, and I will try to add some advice that might be helpful.

Distrust of Self

Distrust of self is humility. It is no accident that humility is the foundation of the whole spiritual life. We are tiny, weak and broken. God is Infinite, all powerful, Truth itself. And He loves us. He wants what is best for us. He has done and continues to do everything we allow Him to do for us to flourish. And our enemies—the world, the flesh and the devil—are much more powerful than we are. So, without humility, without seeking His help first, the whole project is a non-starter. Any house built by us alone is a house built on sand that will be washed away.

Humility is brutal honesty, and brutal honesty includes not just our weakness but our infinite worth. We are worth more to God than the whole physical universe. We are sons and daughters of God. We are all unique, unrepeatable. God has had each of us mind for all of Eternity. He died for each one of us.

So, what does humility look like in the spiritual life? First and foremost, it means obedience. "If you love me, you will keep my commandments" (Jn 14:15). Those who think that all Ten Commandments are suggestions, or not true, are not humble. God Himself wrote these. He knows what He is doing.

Secondly, it means repentance. "[W]hat shall we do? And Peter said to them, 'Repent, and be baptized every one of you'" (Acts 2:37–38). We constantly sin. When we do sin, we need to turn back to God and ask forgiveness. "If we confess our sins, He is faithful and just, and will forgive our sins" (1 Jn 1:9). We must always keep in mind that God's favorite thing to do is forgive sins because sin is what keeps us apart from Him. But He won't do it against our will. He won't do it unless we ask.

Another major aspect of humility is trust—trust in God's Providence. We all have plans and ideas about how things should play out in our lives. These can be large or small. When things don't work out the way we planned we often get angry or anxious or depressed. Distrust of self says: "God has something better for me than what I had planned. He sees the big picture, and how this fits into the plan of my entire life. He knows what He is doing. He wants what is best for me and so I will trust that He will bring good out of this situation as only He can." I was finally able to flip this switch in my head, to some degree, and I can't tell you the peace and freedom that came with it. Elections are no exception. More on this at the end.

Humility extends into every aspect of our lives, because the spiritual life includes every part of our lives. Devotions and spiritual exercises are no exception. Some people get so attached to devotions and traditions (small "t") that they become idols. When it is suggested that they leave them, or a season in life prevents them, they go into a tailspin. This means the real focus was on the devotion and not on God. We are idol making machines. We need to be detached from everything that is not God.

9
Confidence in God

The love of God is trustworthy (Rom 10:13).

God is faithful (1 Cor 1:9).

Hopefully Chapter 4 demonstrated that God is not only trustworthy, but loves us and wants what is best for us. I think that most of us have a general sense that God is good, but what about for me? FOR ME? Is God trustworthy for me? Does He love me? Does He want what is best for me? Will He help me in time of need? Is He watching out for me? Thankfully, the answer is "Yes."

Scripture is filled with "for me" quotes, and what was true for the people quoted in the Bible is true for us as well. Mary says: "for he who is mighty has done great things *for me*" (Lk 1:49). St. Paul says: "I live by faith in the Son of God, who loved me and gave himself *for me*" (Gal 2:20). At the Last Supper Jesus says: "This cup which is poured out *for you* is the new covenant in my blood" (Lk 22:20). Can we have this same confidence in God? What are we to do?

Scupoli gives us a "to do" list. He says that there are four things on our "to do" list when it comes to having confidence in God.[1]

---

[1] Scupoli, *Spiritual Combat*, Ch. 3, 11–13.

First, we need "to ask for [God's help] with great humility."

Second, we need "to contemplate with ardent faith [that] ... to Him, nothing is difficult."

Third, we need to recall witnesses from the Bible (as was noted above).

Fourth, before we do anything, "we should look at our own weakness on the one hand, and on the other contemplate the infinite power, wisdom, and goodness of God."

This is solid advice when we are in times of trouble or temptation. Obviously, it will take time and effort to get into this habit. But the time and effort will pay huge dividends in future trials. We can also remember the words of St. Paul: "I can do all things in him who strengthens me" (Phil 4:13). ALL THINGS!

This is all fine and well on a good day. But what about those who have experienced severe trauma, or will experience it in the future? Where was/is God then? Unfortunately, this scenario of severe trauma is becoming more and more common. The above words from Scupoli and St. Paul seem like cold comfort at best. The feeling of being abandoned by God is real. We have walked for years with someone who has been through this. And the trauma was at the hands of a cleric, making it all the more challenging. What I can tell you is that healing and re-establishing trust with God is not only possible but powerful. After many years of agony, late nights, emotional exhaustion, spiritual darkness, counseling and spiritual direction, she has been truly healed. Not only has she been healed, but she now ministers to victims in similar situations. Interestingly, Scripture paints a similar picture. We read about horrific tragedies that befall people. But that is never the end of the story. God restores, with the restored always in a better place spiritually.

10
Proper Use of Faculties

Human virtues are firm attitudes, stable dispositions, habitual perfections of intellect and will that govern our actions, order our passions, and guide our conduct according to reason and faith (CCC, 1804).

At times I get new patients who come in sheepishly, and it eventually it comes out that they are in recovery from some drug addiction. I always say: "That's great! You are wiser and better off than 90% of the population." They look confused. Then I say: "You have been pushed to admit to others that you are powerless over a certain drug (your main idol), that you need a higher power (God) to regain control, and you were encouraged to make amends to people you have hurt. In reality, this is all of us. Most people are never forced to admit their slavery to an addiction (idol), seek help from God, or make amends for hurting people in the past." The patient immediately breathes a sigh of relief and we move on.

We all have vices; we are all idol-making machines. Original Sin is the great leveler. As Pope Benedict XVI once said: we are all beaten, naked, robbed and left for dead like the man in the Good

Samaritan story.[1] The issue at hand here is what we can do to try to approximate the integrity that Adam and Eve enjoyed in the Garden. Another way to ask this is how do we use each of our faculties—the intellect and will and appetites—the way that God made them to function? Another way to ask this is how do we become virtuous?

If trusting God seems difficult, becoming virtuous seems impossible. The world throws a tidal wave of temptation over us every day. How can one hour of Mass on Sunday even start to compete with temptations of every shape, size, color, and flavor that bombard us every second of every day? The flesh won't stop screaming at us to satisfy some addiction. And if we exert any effort toward virtue, the devil will use any and every trick in his playbook to try to block it.

Daily Duties of our Vocation

First, a big part of the answer was already given. God calls each of us to our own unique vocation because He has designed this plan for us as our road to sainthood. He knows us better than we know ourselves. He knows what we need and He gives us what we need. Now it is our job to cooperate. A huge first step toward virtue is justly and honestly fulfilling all of our duties at home and in the

---

[1] See Pope Benedict XVI, Message for the Twenty First World Day of the Sick (February 11, 2013).

workplace. And our main duty in both places is loving those who God has put in our path. As we all know, this is rarely easy. But love is sacrificial and sacrifice always involves suffering. It means saying "No" to a lot of the things we like to do (excessive screen time, excessive sports, etc.). The "No" helps to redirect our lower faculties to more proper functioning. Doing this faithfully day in and day out carries us a long way along the road of virtue. This only stands to reason as we spend 90% or more of our time and energy fulfilling our vocation.

Love is located in the will, so growing in love as we fulfill our vocation is a proper use of the will. We use our intellect at home and in the workplace, often at home more than in the workplace. We need to use our intellect for creative solutions to problems and to avoid moral dilemmas. In short, what is needed is the proper ordering and use of our faculties.

Sacraments

Second, we need to frequent the sacraments. We cannot be faithful to our vocation without God's Grace. Cannot. I know people who do not frequent the sacraments but appear to be fulfilling their vocations very well, and they seem to be quite virtuous. But they cannot love those around them the way God wants us to love them without the love of God in them. "Without Me, you can do nothing" (Jn 15:5). We bear no fruit if we are not connected to the vine.

Spiritual Exercises

Third, we need a routine of spiritual exercises. What do we do with our free time? What do we do with the little time and energy we have left at the end of the day/week? This becomes the million-dollar question. Clearly, we need some form of recreation (re-creation, not mere entertainment, although there is a time and place for entertainment). Our focus here is on habits that make proper use of our faculties.

I am going to use the term "spiritual exercises" somewhat loosely here. A formal look at these can be found in a book called *A Theology of Spiritual Exercises* by Douglas Bushman.

There are many spiritual exercises that properly direct the intellect. Studying Church teaching or studying the Faith is something that all of us should be doing regularly (to some degree). We cannot love what we do not know. We need to deepen our knowledge of God and His Church in order to better love Him. Regular reading of the Bible is most important. God is the Author of Scripture. Every other author is second rate, and the Bible is a living Word. God speaks to us as directly today as He spoke on earth two thousand years ago. Some people say they never hear God speaking to them. All they have to do is open the Bible and God will speak to them. Spiritual reading is also helpful here, including the lives of the saints and inspirational works. Reading the lives of the saints is so helpful to me because I see how many of them struggled in the same ways I do.

Daily examination of conscience is extremely important. Every night we should review the day. Where did we do it right? Where did we go wrong? What were the circumstances? How can we avoid sin in the future? How can we better call on God's help when we need it?

Some spiritual exercises can help us to love more perfectly. Service activities, penances and spiritual friendships can expand our love by focusing on others rather than ourselves.

The Body

Up until now we have focused on our spiritual faculties: intellect and will. Now we can turn our attention to the body. We talk about the seven wonders of the ancient world. The human body is *the* wonder of the universe. It is by far the most complex thing in the universe. There are brilliant minds who spend a lifetime studying one tiny aspect of the human body. As time goes on, we realize how much more complex the body is, even as we understood it just a few years ago (gut biome as one example). Indeed, we are "Beautifully and wonderfully made" (Ps 139:14). And, if we are in a state of Grace, we are indeed a Temple of the Holy Spirit. We should be thankful for our bodies for all these reasons, plus the fact that despite all that can go wrong, things usually go right.

Unfortunately, since Original Sin, our bodies have become disordered and often turn against us:

> The entire spiritual warfare, consequently, consists in this: the rational [spiritual] faculty is placed between the divine will above it and the sensitive appetite [body] below it, and is attacked from both sides - God moving it by His grace, and the flesh by its appetites strive for victory.[2]

If you don't believe this author, let us hear St Paul:

> For I know that nothing good dwells within me, that is, in my flesh. I can will what is right, but I cannot do it. For I do not do the good I want, but the evil I do not want is what I do (Rom 7:18–19).

This is the great St. Paul! The battle for God and against sin is fierce. It is every day. It is day and night. And our disordered lower appetites are not our friends here.

If you are anything like me your body is screaming at you 24/7. I am tired all day, then I can't sleep. I'm hungry all day, I eat all day, I

---

[2] Scupoli, *Spiritual Combat*, Ch. 12, 33.

overeat due to stress, which makes me more tired. Every morning I promise myself I won't stay up late watching movies. Then every night I am up late watching movies. Every day I do what I do not want to do.

How do we break this cycle? How do we develop discipline when we feel as though we have none?

First, we need to do what St. Paul did, which is what I mentioned earlier. We need to admit that we are powerless and turn to God for help. In many ways these addictions and weaknesses are a great blessing, for all of the reasons I mentioned in my testimony. They are remedies for pride (if we allow them to be and don't identify with them) among other things. In the spiritual realm, pride is a worse sin than physical addiction. I know many former addicts who are much closer to God than are many college professors I know.

Second, we need help from others. Left to our own devices, many of us never make progress. It is wonderful that God made us in such a way that we really do need each other.

Third, pain can be helpful here. Pain is a wonderful thing because it tells us that something is wrong. It is a warning signal for us to do something differently. I love drinking alcohol, but now it makes me extremely tired. I can't get done in a day what I need to get done if I drink too much the night before. So, I don't.

What we need is discipline, whether it comes from God or anywhere else, we need discipline.

Fasting

All of this is a long way of saying that fasting is necessary. Interestingly, the world has caught up to the Church in this regard. Usually, the world takes ideas from the Church and perverts them. Modern concepts of justice, love, care for the sick, university systems, etc., have all been taken from the Church and distorted from their original meaning. But the world has now taken up fasting as a new fad. And they have much to add in the way of tips, advice, strategies, options, etc. And the list of benefits is long, not only to our physical health but to our mental health as well. And that is from the world. Unfortunately, they don't see the great spiritual benefits in addition. So, their help here can be useful. The point is, we have to do some sort of fasting. We need our eating to be disciplined at times to some degree. A good boxer is a hungry boxer, as the old saying goes.

I hate fasting and I don't do it well. I used to do it well, but I have gotten much weaker over time. A key concept in the spiritual life is to be flexible. We cannot be too attached to anything that is not God. Life changes. Life happens. Circumstances change.

Another key concept in the spiritual life is the law of gradualness. This applies to nearly every aspect of the spiritual life. Slow growth is real growth as they say. Very few of us will be like St. Paul and have an instant conversion. And after a conversion or reversion, very few of us will be ready or able to go to daily Mass and then spend two more hours a day doing our formal spiritual exercises. Nobody goes from being a couch potato to being an Olympic athlete, so going from no fasting to a full day fast usually doesn't go well. If we usually eat a high carb diet, fasting will be even more difficult. Tips and strategies will be helpful here.

I would make a suggestion here. We are weak, our lives are chaotic, and life is more complicated now than ever before. I think that a good start to fasting would be giving up processed food, snacking between meals, alcohol, and screen time on fast days. You can eat what you want, as long as it is something that God gave us (normal, natural food). This is one strategy among many, but I think people would go a long way toward the discipline of fasting with this approach.

I said that we are weak. Almost every aspect of our modern, Western culture is unhealthy. As I said earlier, in the past—and not so distant past—most people were farmers. We were built to be farmers. Farmers get up when the sun comes up. They do physical work all day long outside in the sun. They eat fresh, local natural food. They go to bed when the sun goes down and there is no insomnia. They are exposed to microbes all day long, which helps their immune system. They are in tune with the cycles of nature, not just daily but yearly as well. They have much less work in the winter, when the days are shorter, so they have a yearly season of rest.

We often get up before the sun gets up with an alarm clock. Most of us have indoor, sedentary jobs. We often eat unhealthy and artificial food. Even many of the natural foods that we eat have been transported a great distance and need to be artificially preserved. Much of this food is also covered or filled with pesticides and herbicides. Most of our food is depleted of nutrients, and the nutrients that we do eat are malabsorbed due to a disrupted gut biome. The toxins that are not supposed to be absorbed are absorbed because of an inflamed gut lining. Our water is filled with toxins, including microplastics. We are daily exposed to household chemicals. We have electric lights and so are able to stay up long past sundown. Our sleep is insufficient and disordered. And there is no seasonal rest built into our schedules. The list could go on but you get the point. It is no wonder that fatigue, depression, and anxiety are epidemic. We hardly stand a chance.

I will list just a few proofs that we are weak. Sperm counts are half of what they were thirty years ago. Testosterone levels in men are much less than half of what they were eighty years ago. Asthma and allergies are epidemic, indicating disordered immune systems. Most mental health diagnoses are rising and reaching crisis levels. And none of this takes into account the extreme spiritual darkness all around us that St. John Paul II called the "culture of death."

All of this is to say that fasting in our current condition should look different than what it looked like for St. Francis of Assisi. I will repeat, using different words, that in my opinion, we would be well served if our fasting consisted of a healthy lifestyle. Exercise most if not all days of the week, with two days including exercise as rigorous as we are able. Make good food choices and use a veggie wash on fruits and vegetables that we don't peel. Filter our water. Get adequate sleep. Spend time outdoors most if not all days of the week. Take a probiotic regularly. These can be types of fasting and at the same time a proper use of our physical faculties.

Imagination

No book on the spiritual life would be complete without addressing the imagination. The imagination is one of our physical faculties, so it is not part of the intellect or will. Because it is part of our physical nature, Satan can influence it. And influence it he does. The imagination is one of the most contested battle grounds in the spiritual life. The battle here seems almost constant. What are we to do?

The term for control or discipline here is custody of the thoughts. How do we keep custody of a wild animal? First and foremost, we need to stay faithful to all of the spiritual exercises noted above. These will keep us focused on the good and not evil. Second, we need to keep custody of the eyes. We need to take care of what we choose to see. Third, we have a simple and powerful weapon that we can use here (as well as with all temptations). I think the Jesus prayer is one of the most underused weapons in the whole of the spiritual battle. All we have to do is say: "Jesus, Jesus, Jesus." When we say the Holy Name of Jesus, we make Him present. And when He is present, the demons flee. This will also help us to recollect, as we will discuss in the section on prayer.

It is insightful to hear what Scupoli has to say about lust. He treats it differently than the other temptations. He is referring to one-on-one encounters with people, but we can extrapolate to the imagination here. "Not even the fear of the flames of hell will be able to master the fury of the sensual fires enkindled in your heart. Look for safety, then, in flight. There is no other way to escape."[3] Other temptations we can face head-on.

---

[3] Scupoli, *Spiritual Combat*, Ch. 9, 54.

Lust is like quicksand: the longer you attend to it, even if you are trying to fight it, the more it drags you in. With regard to the imagination, you need to run from it through the Jesus prayer, recollection, or any other method that works for you.

11
Prayer

Those who pray will be saved.
Those who do not pray will not be saved.
                              St. Alphonsus de Liguori

The "spiritual battle" of the Christian's new life is inseparable from the battle of prayer (CCC, 2725).

Personal Relationship

Why is prayer so critical? The whole goal of the spiritual life is to live in union with God. This union with God will never be complete on earth, but will be perfect and glorious in Heaven. Those in Heaven are "divinized," meaning they become God-like. That is because in Heaven we are physically and spiritually in union with Christ. We fully participate in the Body of Christ; we enter into the very life of God Himself. We have no images to describe how glorious it is. "What no eye has seen, nor ear heard, nor heart of man conceived, what God has prepared for those who love Him" (1 Cor 2:9). That is why Scripture calls Heaven a wedding banquet. The marriage union here on earth is meant to be a type or model or precursor of our marital union with Christ in Heaven. Just as the two become one here in marriage, we will become one with Christ in Heaven. We will become part of the Infinite and

Eternal. This is why Satan hates marriage and is savagely attacking it right now.

Our goal is to be united to a Person, to be "married" to a Person. How can we be united to someone if we don't know him or her? And how do we get to know them without talking with them? There is not much of a relationship with someone you don't talk with. Why would we even want to go to Heaven if we have no idea Who we will be with? Why would we want to spend Eternity with a stranger? God will never force anyone into Heaven. Everyone in Heaven is someone with whom God wants to be and who wants to be with God. It is not simply a luxury spa where we go to rest and relax. Heaven is a relationship, a marriage-like relationship. And, there are no forced marriages with God.

This is why prayer is essential to get to Heaven. The relationship with God for all Eternity starts on Earth. There are some saints who got married (went to Heaven) after their first date with God. There were pagan Roman soldiers who saw the way that Christians faced death and immediately requested the same martyrdom. The good thief is another example. But most of us have not faced that scenario, at least not yet. Most of the saints lived as Christians for many years. The goal of Christian life is greater and greater union with God. Greater union requires prayer, conversing with your future Spouse.

We will stay with the marriage analogy because that is the one that God uses. Think of a blind date, second date, more dates, courtship, engagement, marriage. What we say, how we say it, ease in speech, etc., all progress and mature as our relationship grows deeper in love. The same is true with prayer. The types of prayer will hopefully make this clearer. We need to remember that each type of prayer grows deeper and becomes more meaningful the closer we get to God.

Vocal Prayer

Any human conversation, including our conversation with God, entails words. These words can be expressed either *exteriorly*, verbally or vocally, or *interiorly*, i.e., silently, as if "spoken" within the recesses of our hearts. The exterior or vocal expression of prayer can happen in in public or in private. The words themselves may be the same, as in praying the "Our Father," but we can say these words either with others or alone.

The distinction between public and private vocal prayer is evident in the life of Jesus as well. At times, Jesus is seen and heard praying in public, as in the synagogue, at the tomb of Lazarus, or among His disciples.[1] At other times, the gospels

---

[1] See Lk 4:14–21; Jn 11:41–42; Jn 17.

writers record that Jesus went off by Himself to pray.[2]

The Church has followed our Lord's example, and Her public prayer is found within Her "liturgy," most especially, the Holy Eucharist or Mass. The Mass is the perfect public prayer because we literally enter into the Paschal mystery. We discussed this earlier. The Family dimension of the Church is visibly and audibly present here. The Eucharist unites us with Jesus and unites us with every member of His Church. This visible unity signifies our spiritual unity with God and each other. It is a foretaste of Heaven.

Public prayers are very powerful for intercession and very good for us spiritually. They build up the Church and change history. St. Dominic was a failure for years until Mary gave him the Rosary. He became an overnight success after praying it. The victory at the Battle of Lepanto is another example of how praying the Rosary changed history. These prayers should be part of our everyday Christian life.

Public prayer, however, presupposes and depends upon what the faithful do in the privacy of their own rooms. Their private prayer may resemble public prayer in many ways except that it is done, well, alone,[3] and alone the prayerful can recite

---

[2] See, e.g., Mt 14:13; 14:23; Mk 1:35; 6:46; Lk 5:16.
[3] See Mt 6:6.

familiar vocal prayers or enter into the silence of their hearts.

Mental Prayer

Again, prayer can happen either exteriorly and vocally, in public settings or in private, or our conversation with God can be silent or "spoken" within the recesses of our hearts. This interior or mental form of prayer is known as either meditation or contemplation. The former describes the kind of prayer that benefits from a deliberate study of and meditation on Sacred Scripture or the writings of the saints, doctors and theologians of the Church. Meditation, the *Catechism* reminds us, "is a prayerful quest engaging thought, imagination, emotion, and desire. Its goal is to make our own in faith the subject considered, by confronting it with the reality of our own life" (*CCC*, 2723). Of the two forms of mental prayer, meditation is perhaps the most important, even if it is not the most intense. In meditation, the faithful learn to speak, study, search, and listen to God in the life of His Son, in the lives of His "holy ones," and in his or her own life.

For most of my life, until very recently, I was only capable of Mass and these vocal prayers. God understands. He knows us better than we know ourselves.

Meditative Prayer

As I said, the first form of mental prayer is meditative prayer. Years ago, a priest told me that if we had to choose between daily Mass or meditative prayer, we should choose meditative prayer. I didn't believe him. In all my years learning theology we heard that the Eucharist is the "source and summit of the Christian life." How could meditative prayer be better than that? In his explanation he said that you can go to Mass and recite your vocal prayers while keeping God at arm's length. With meditative prayer there is no arm's length. You are one-on-one with God and having a personal conversation with Him. You don't have to use your own words or bear your soul at Mass. Meditative prayer is up close and personal. There is no hiding.

Deep down inside I thought he might be right, because I trusted him. But I didn't want to believe him because I thought I was unable to do meditative prayer. I gave you my testimony. I felt there is no way that I could sit alone, quiet, for fifteen or more minutes and talk to Someone I couldn't see.

Maybe I could have; maybe I couldn't have. We will never know. But I did have a breakthrough at age fifty-eight. A trusted theologian encouraged me. Then I read that Teresa of Avila once said, "This method [meditative or mental prayer] should be the beginning, the middle and the end of prayer for all of us."[4] The great master of prayer is basically saying that this is like eating and sleeping. We all have to do this every day, no matter what. This is the hub of the whole wheel of prayer. But how do we begin?

Another breakthrough came when I learned that the imagination plays a big part in meditative prayer. I wanted to get tips from other people, so I started asking what their meditative prayer looks like. It turns out that very few people do this. And for those who do meditative prayer, there are no two ways that even closely resemble each other in how they talk to God one on one. I think it's wonderful that God's relationship with each of His children is so different, so unique.

The Chosen TV series helped me with respect to my imagination. God is Infinite and has no body. How on earth am I supposed to use my imagination to picture Him? Well, it turns out that God does have a physical body. And it looks a lot like Jesus. "Philip said to Him, 'Lord, show us the Father' . . . Jesus said to him . . . 'He who has seen me has seen the Father'" (Jn 14: 8–9).

The Chosen has helped me to picture Jesus not as the sanitized stoic He is often portrayed as. On earth, He was real. His hands and feet were dirty. His countenance was different from ours, but He

---

[4] Marie-Eugene, *I Want to See God*, 65.

spoke and still speaks to us at our level and with our language.

When I sit down to do meditative prayer, I picture Jesus during His ministry sitting on a log at night near the campfire. He is there by Himself and I approach Him. Every morning He says the same thing to me: "Matt, I've missed you. Come here and talk to Me." From there the conversation can go in any direction. I usually start with whatever is on my mind. I have no idea day to day where He is going to go, but it is a different direction every day. I usually end in tears, but they are good tears.

In a million years I never thought that this was remotely possible for me, but God can do all things. ALL THINGS. And if He can do this with me, He can do this with anyone. All we have to do is give Him a little time and attention.

As you can imagine, there are many challenges at the beginning. The awkwardness of a first date is always an issue, but you can't fall in love unless you start with a first date. The world, the flesh, and the devil will all be screaming at you not to do this. If you don't believe me, just try it. But I will beg you to persevere. What Teresa of Avila said is true: we need to do this every day. Exceptions would include the house burning down.

The world will bombard you with a thousand other things to do, and all of them will seem immediately urgent. But think of it this way: all 168 hours in the week are a gift from God to you. All

He's asking is for fifteen minutes each day. You can do it. The rest of the day will be more peaceful and productive because you can turn back to Him any minute of the day. You can continue your conversation. You can tell Him how much you need His help, and it will be there. If not, He will console you. He will give you what you need at the moment, and it will be personal.

Recollection

Going back to Jesus and talking to Him throughout the day is called recollection. I have friends who have mentioned recollection for years, but I had no idea what they were talking about. Recollection is returning your mind to the presence of God. You can do this any time, day or night, in any situation. It is most helpful during times of temptation.

Temptation

The flesh will make known to you every desire you have ever known as soon as you try to meditate. If you weren't hungry before, you will suddenly be hungry. You will be thirsty, tired, etc. Please persevere.

A story here may be helpful. I have prayed to Mother Mary since I was a child. I have always felt close to her but, every once in a while, there is a nagging thought: Should I just go to Jesus instead?

I was tempted by lust during meditation. Jesus then brought me to the crowning with thorns. He was sitting, all bloodied, all by Himself, on a small rock stool. The crown of thorns was on His head. I was standing a short distance with a stick in my hand. The lustful thoughts would have been me hitting Him in the head. I begged Him to stop me, but He wouldn't. He wouldn't look at me or say anything or do anything to stop me. I started moving toward Him when Mary appeared. She stood right in front of me, and kindly asked me to stop. What He told me with this image was that He will do nothing, nothing, to get in the way of my free will. I am free to do whatever I want and He will not interfere. But Mary can help us in times of temptation. The lesson for me is to never stop asking Mary for help, especially in times of temptation.

The devil can be very distracting during meditative prayer. If you doubt the value of meditative prayer, just start doing it. Every temptation you have ever known will come to mind. God allows the devil to influence our imagination, as we have said. But he cannot influence the intellect or will. The Jesus prayer is very helpful here: Simply say: "Jesus, Jesus, Jesus." You can keep repeating this as many times as you want.

A trusted theologian gave me an image of meditative prayer that is very helpful. When we have a developed interior life, God has home field advantage. When we are practicing meditative prayer, God has home field advantage. God meets us, personally, in our heart. The heart is at the depths of our soul. We can have a deeply personal relationship with God to the degree/extent that we spend time in the depth of our soul, when we turn our attention to Him there. The devil has home field advantage whenever we avoid our interior life, our heart.

Personal Relationship with Christ

I will conclude by saying that meditative prayer is the Catholic version of "a personal relationship with Christ." It is deeply personal.

12
Polycrisis

My Father, if it be possible, let this cup pass from me; nevertheless, not as I will but as thou wilt (Mt 26:39).

Polycrisis is a secular term. It describes a situation where overlapping crises are happening at the same time. I mention this because, at the time of this writing, our world seems to be descending into this rather quickly. Economic systems around the world are on the verge of collapse. Some world leaders seem to want WWIII; many, at least, predict the metastasis of current wars. National borders in the West are almost nonexistent. Our streets are getting more violent. Crime is up. Morality is down. Pornography is a cancer rotting our culture from within. We still kill one million innocents each year by abortion in the U.S. alone. Political divisions are irreconcilable and seen as existential threats by both sides.

 I mention all of this not because of world events alone. More and more people and families that we know are living under the burden of a polycrisis personally. Economic insecurity at the same time that parents are sick and children are in trouble and the marriage is strained and then someone has a serious injury. Life seems overwhelming with no light at the end of the tunnel. What can we do for relief, or at least guidance?

Hopefully at least some of the advice I have already given will be helpful. After frequenting the sacraments, my best advice is daily meditative prayer, and I have found meditation on the four last things to be extremely helpful. It gives us an Eternal perspective, but also better enables us to abandon ourselves to God's Providential care. The four last things are death, judgement, Heaven and Hell. In other words, meditating on Eternity. There are only two zip codes in Eternity: Heaven and Hell. As we have said, Eternity is FOREVER. We would do very well to take time thinking about where we want to spend forever.

The Four Last Things

The best resource in this area is a book called *Preparation for Death* by St. Alphonsus de Liguori.[1] I read this book many years ago, but I seemed to have forgotten his advice. My wife and I know what it is to be overwhelmed in life. Unfortunately, most of us tend to forget much of what we have learned when the issues at hand are very pressing. The good news is that God can make up for all that we are lacking. The Holy Spirit

---

[1] Alphonsus de Liguori, *Preparation for Death; or, Considerations on the Eternal Truths*, ed. Eugene Grimm (Brooklyn, NY: Redemptorist Fathers, 1926).

reminded me of this advice during one of the recent election cycles. I had been following politics very closely for about twenty years. And every single day during those twenty years I was angry about something political. One day the Holy Spirit told me to think of the four last things. I did, and I have done so (though now mostly subconsciously) every day since. It has changed my life tremendously for the better.

Heaven

This is just my style, but I skip over death and judgement because they are implied in the last two. I have already tried to describe Heaven: it is a new Heaven and a new Earth. By that I mean spiritualized. Think of how limited our bodies are now. Think of Jesus' body after the Resurrection: He was not limited by time or space, He could walk through walls, He could be wherever He wanted to be by simply wanting to be there. We will be like that, but so too will everything around us be spiritualized. The colors will be more beautiful and brighter. The smells will be perfect for us personally (like the manna in the desert). There will be no pain, no form of suffering. We will be in glorious union with all the other saints. But best of all we will behold God face-to-face. God IS beauty. Everything in Heaven is good. God IS good. We will have supernatural, infused knowledge. God IS truth. And we will be doing perfectly what we were made to do—love. God IS love. And we will be in perfect union with Him.

I am better able to endure suffering when I can see this light at the end of the tunnel.

Hell

Then there is the other eternal zip code. Hell is a horrific place, and it is far from empty. Listen to Jesus: "Enter by the narrow gate; for the gate is wide and the way is easy, that leads to destruction, and those who enter it are many" (Mt 7:13-14). The seers at Fatima personally witnessed multitudes falling into Hell. Many other saints confirm their words. It is true that a good and loving God would never send anyone to Hell. It is also true that everyone in Hell is there by their own free choice. It is also true that God would never force anyone into Heaven. All in Heaven are there by free choice.

Just as there is no way we can imagine the glory of Heaven, there is no way we can imagine the horror of Hell. St Alphonsus guides us. It is dark, except for the flashes of hideous faces of demons torturing you. The sounds are screams of cursing and agony; it is at a deafening volume. The stench is so bad that if one damned soul came to earth, we would all die.[2] The equivalent of sulfuric acid is

---

[2] Liguori, *Preparation for Death*, 264.

being constantly poured down your throat. There is terrible hunger and thirst. You are on fire, inside and out, but you don't die. You cannot move. But the torture of the five senses is not the worst pain. The worst pain is the loss of Heaven, the loss of God, the loss of our ability to do what we were made to do—love. The "principal torment, his hell, will be the pain of loss, or that pain arising from having lost God."[3] There is no love in Hell. Everyone hates each other. That is another form of torture. Worse, you know it was the result of your free choices that brought you there. So, your conscience is tortured as well. Nobody sent you there.

In the midst of my anger about certain politicians, I was inspired to think of Heaven and Hell. I don't want Hell for anyone, even my worst enemy, so instead of getting angry with them I began to pray for them. The flip of this switch has transformed my life. It didn't occur to me at the time, but this was actually an act of obedience. Jesus told us to pray for our enemies.[4] This seems like the hardest message of Christianity. Hopefully it helps our enemies. It does wonderful things for us.

---

[3] Ibid., 262.
[4] See Mt 5:44.

Surrender to God's Will

There is a corollary to all of this; actually, to the whole book. The corollary is: "We know that in everything God works for good with those who love him" (Rom 8:28). If it is true that God has known everything for all Eternity, and if it is true that He has had each of us in mind for all Eternity, and if it is true that He put us in this time and in this place as part of His Eternal plan, then everything that befalls us can work for our good (if we allow it to be so). That means that any and all suffering in our lives can be used for good (ours and the good of others).

There is an excellent little spiritual book that helps us to see the Hand of Divine Providence in every aspect of our lives, and to conform our will to God's will in all times and places. I found it extremely helpful. It is called *Into Your Hands Father* by Wilfrid Stinissen.[5] As a Carmelite, he is fully steeped in the Carmelite tradition. Much of what he does systematizes St Thérèse of the Little Flower and dovetails on the spiritual classic *Abandonment to Divine Providence* by Father Jean Pierre de Caussade. The following quotation will help explain:

> The Gospels and spiritual literature point out various practices of importance on the journey to God.... All of these things have

---

[5] Wilfrid Stinissen, *Into Your Hands Father. Abandoning Ourselves to the God Who Loves Us* (San Francisco: Ignatius Press, 2011).

> their place ..., but they cause us to feel confused and divided.... What we need most is a central idea .... In my opinion that central idea is surrender.[6]

By surrender he means surrendering to God's will at all times and in all places. It means trusting in God's plan for our lives even if it would not be our first choice. It means trusting that God's plan for our life is better than our plan for our life. It means trusting that all of our suffering can be used for our good and the good of others.

A comment must be made here about God's Will. God can never will evil. He can never desire us to suffer. We call this God's active will. But God does allow evil, He allows us to suffer. But He only allows us to suffer so that greater good will come of that suffering. That greater good could be for ourselves or for others or for both. We may never see that greater good until we get to Heaven. But we need to trust that we will see it. We call this God's passive will, Him allowing evil.

Personally, I cannot surrender to God's will in all circumstances unless I have my eyes on Eternity. If I am thinking only of the here and now, I am easily thrown off balance. And my three enemies (the world, the flesh, and the devil) who are stronger than me have an easy time getting me to sin. I am happy to say that thoughts of Eternity and Divine

---

[6] Stinissen, *Into Your Hands Father*, 9.

Providence are now in my subconscious. I don't have to consciously think of them. My mind goes there like a reflex whenever adversity strikes or I hear bad news. I am hoping to mature in meditative prayer so that recollection will also be there reflexively.

Trust in Divine Providence, trusting that God knows better than I do, has completely transformed my way of thinking. This is one aspect of the mind renewal that God wants us to have.[7] It is a great source of peace in times of crisis.

---

[7] See Rom 12:2.

13
Hope

For in this hope we were saved (Rom 8:24).

God always ends with hope. All of the Old Testament prophets started with doom and gloom and ended in hope. We will do likewise.

Hope seems to be the virtue most lacking right now, both in the Church and in the world. The previous chapter identified some of the causes of this hopelessness. There are many others, not the least of which is the Darwinistic culture we are currently enduring. Materialistic atheism leaves people without hope.

Trust God's Plan

We have at least three major reasons for hope. The first is trust in God's Providential plan, as we have been discussing. During COVID I ministered to hundreds of people. One of the many lines I repeated was that "God only allows evil so that greater good will come of it. I am squinting very hard and I can't see it right now." Well, now that we all have more perspective, we are able to see at least some of the good. There have been many conversions and reversions since. And many who have not done so have woken up to realize that the culture of death really is dark (though they may not use those exact words). We in the West have been anesthetized by instant entertainment, lots of tasty calories and nonstop distraction. Most people's lives are actually devoid of any meaning. People are starting to look for real meaning in their lives—not only in religion but in human relationships. The point is that God has a plan. It is often hard for us to see it, and sometimes we never do on this side of the Veil. Not only does God have a plan but it is a good one. It is the best one. Our calling is to trust in that plan and stay close to Him. If we do, we can be very hopeful.

We also have to remember that the Church often thrives in adversity and grows cold in times of prosperity. Personally, I think that, if we were not living in such challenging times, I would be a mediocre Christian at best.

Grace

Second, where sin abounds, Grace abounds more.[1] Sin is certainly abounding. We need to trust in God's abounding Grace, and we need to beg for it every day. We need to be confident in hope that our prayers will be answered. If you want visible proof of this abundant Grace, follow Dr. Bob Schuchts for a week, or a month. He runs the John Paul II Healing Center.[2] He witnesses countless miracles

---

[1] See Rom 5:20–1.
[2] See: https://jpiihealingcenter.org/.

on every retreat he gives. I know. I have been on two of them.

Divine Mercy

Third, we are in an age of Mercy. God revealed this to the world through St. Faustina in the 1930s. The Divine Mercy devotions are very powerful. They are explained in her Diary. For many of us, reading the Diary is more consoling than the Bible. It doesn't add anything to the Bible, but it highlights, underscores, and puts an exclamation point on God's Mercy. The promises are over-the-top. God says that the greatest sinners have the greatest claim on His Mercy. He says that all of the sins of all mankind are like a tiny drop in His ocean of Mercy. He says that the conversion of sinners is the prayer He loves most to answer. Etc.

This is wonderful at many levels. Why did God wait so long to reveal this devotion? Because we need it now more than ever. Never before in human history has there been an atheistic culture. But God has not abandoned us. He is not looking at us wondering what we will do next. He is like the father in the Prodigal Son parable whose heart was aching while his son was away, and He is offering every good gift in overabundance.

In reality, Divine Mercy is the only hope that humanity has ever had. The only thing that can separate us from God is sin. We were made for God, so our goal is union with God. The only way we can be happy is with God. So, the problem is sin, and we are unable to get rid of past sins or to stop sinning now on our own. We need God. In His Mercy He forgives sin. His favorite thing to do is to forgive sin, because sin is what keeps us apart from Him. And He can't stand being apart from us. So, Mercy is our only hope, and it is now more abundant than ever.

"For the sake of His sorrowful Passion, have mercy on us and on the whole world."

About the Author

Matthew Paquette, MD, MTS is married with four children. He and his wife Mary practice medicine in an NFP only general practice. In addition to his medical degree, Matthew has a Master degree in pastoral theology from the University of Dallas in Irving, Texas.

Printed in the USA
CPSIA information can be obtained
at www.ICGtesting.com
CBHW030118221024
16170CB00001B/6